# THE CHESTER MYSTERY PLAYS

# THE CHESTER
# MYSTERY PLAYS

### SEVENTEEN PAGEANT PLAYS FROM
### THE CHESTER CRAFT CYCLE

*Adapted into Modern English*

*by*

## MAURICE HUSSEY

**SECOND EDITION**

## HEINEMANN EDUCATIONAL BOOKS

LONDON

Heinemann Educational Books Ltd
22 Bedford Square, London WC1B 3HH

LONDON  EDINBURGH  MELBOURNE  AUCKLAND
HONG KONG  SINGAPORE  KUALA LUMPUR  NEW DELHI
IBADAN  NAIROBI  JOHANNESBURG  KINGSTON
EXETER (NH)  PORT OF SPAIN

ISBN 0 435 23415 3

THIS VERSION OF THE PLAYS
FIRST PUBLISHED IN THE DRAMA LIBRARY 1957
REPRINTED 1960, 1964, 1967, 1971
SECOND EDITION 1975
REPRINTED 1979

FOR
BRYAN HARRIS

Printed and bound in Great Britain by
Morrison & Gibb Ltd, London and Edinburgh

# CONTENTS

# PREFACE

IN preparing this version of the Chester cycle I have read
a number of books upon the medieval drama, a few of which
are noted at the end of the Introduction. The text is based
upon that published by the Early English Text Society, and
I have read in addition an older and freer version in modern
language by I. and O. Bolton King, but except on a few
occasions, where defeated by archaisms or perverse rhyming
in the original, I have attempted to keep closer to the original
vocabulary, while at the same time producing a text without
footnotes. For reading an earlier version and making detailed
comments upon it I am deeply grateful to my friend, Dr. A. I.
Doyle.

The revisions called for in the preparation of a second
edition have been in the interests of bringing the introductory
matter up to date and clarifying the essential theology that
underlies the cycle as a whole. I have added one more play,
*The Temptation*. From the continuing interest of drama
groups in mystery plays both for winter indoor and summer
outdoor performance it is particularly noteworthy that what
was quite adventurous in the 1950s in the form of religious
drama is now common. During that time I have been able to
see performances of all four principal cycles at least once
myself and there is every chance that, once again after many
centuries, the earliest English plays may develop, expand and
continue as if Queen Elizabeth I had never objected to them,
called the texts in and banned them.

The cover depicts the 'Creation' scene from the Holkham
Hall Bible manuscript and is reproduced by kind permission
of the British Library Board.

M. P. H.

Cambridge, 1974

vi

# INTRODUCTION

JUST as it is virtually impossible for us to realise the impact of such events in medieval England as the Black Death or the long civil wars, it is also difficult to have any real understanding of the mystery plays which were happier illuminations of the same scene. We probably imagine that we are familiar with the plays if we have ever seen a nativity play, but it is impossible for us to bring a medieval mind to bear upon the drama and, unless we have seen a representation of a whole cycle, we cannot estimate the impact of these entertainments upon the whole population. It is impossible, for a start, for us to act them in the original manner. We should need to build heavy double-decker carriages on wheels and push them through the streets for three days each summer, to stop traffic and commerce in order to release everybody to act or watch as the long cycle unfolds.

To return more decisively to the medieval festivals. In 1311, after much delay, the Church instituted the feast of Corpus Christi as a spectacular processional celebration. It might have been more fitting to acknowledge the Real Presence of Christ on the anniversary of the Last Supper but Holy Week was already the occasion of much ceremonial and a later date allowed freer scope. In England, at this time, the Church and local authorities collected together plays which commemorated specific anniversaries as well as those which had no such recurrent dates and coherent cycles of plays were established. Local custom was allowed to prevail where a different date was more convenient and, still bearing the title of Corpus Christi plays, the Chester Cycle was later presented at Whitsun and the performances at Lincoln held back till St. Anne's day, July 26th. In the words of Pope Urban IV the new feast was a time when " we both rejoice amid pious weeping and weep amid reverent rejoicing," a good emotional formula on which to base a cycle of biblical plays and give them humanity, divinity and unity.

Though indeed the plays may be interpreted as bridges across which the uneducated could reach religious truths they were more than living visual aids. In their simplest state they fulfilled the requirements of Urban IV so well that there grew up the unwarranted superstition that the person who saw the Risen Christ would not die that same year. At its lowest a play cycle thus became a kind of insurance policy while, at its highest, it was a valid means of grace (ecclesiastically termed a *sacramental* or minor ceremonial) in which all participants had a share if they behaved worthily: not so much as interacting groups of performer and audience but celebrant and congregation.

Considering the medieval drama from our own standpoint in time we find at work in its history the classic antagonism between the Catholic and Protestant interpretations of faith. In the Catholic conception we have room for rituals of every sort: Candlemas Day, Palm Sunday and Holy Week are full of them; over the period of the Nativity there still rules the Crib. The Christmas story continues to engage the minds of dramatists who still treat the event as one suitable for external objective show. The Easter narrative, theologically more significant, is not portrayed in the same manner with any frequency. At this time of the year we turn perhaps towards Protestant music, to the concert-hall to hear one of Bach's *Passions*.

In the Chester cycle we have the prototype of the English mysteries, not subjected to endless revisions and without much peasant comedy which changed some plays from the religious drama into folk drama. There are additions to the biblical story, local touches, realistic sequences which endeared the plays to their audiences, and also theological additions which their author learned from *The Golden Legend* and the Book of James the Less, known as *Protevangelion*, anachronisms obvious as when Noah invokes Christ, and English localisations such as the shepherd's Lancashire oatcake, which serve to remind us that to God all time is one and human salvation a never-ending process. The Chester setting

dates from the fourth quarter of the fourteenth century when
it was translated from Anglo-Norman or French. Ultimately
the cycle came from the earlier efforts of the Church to begin a
dramatic presentation of religion inside its own walls in
its own language. " *Quem quaeritis*? " recited the clergy upon
one side of the choir taking the part of the Angel at the
Tomb after the resurrection, " Whom do you seek? " Those
opposite responded in the words of the three Maries, and
were finally told, " *Surrexit, non est hic;* he has risen, he is not
here." In this scene, the *Quem quaeritis* sequence, is the seed
of all Western theatre, and in the present cycle we have the
earliest version of it in the vernacular.

When we discuss medieval religious plays we must realise
that there were three types with individual differences:

*Liturgical drama:* plays performed in Latin and possibly
later in English in churches.

*Miracle drama:* plays devoted to saints lives such as St.
Nicholas and St. George. Only plays upon Mary Magdalene
and St. Paul remain and are sometimes called Saints' Plays.

*Morality drama:* plays which show man in his fight with
temptation, hesitation and doubt, which mix human beings
with abstractions upon the stage and had the greatest influence
upon the art-drama of the Elizabethan period.

Although Elizabeth I stopped the performances of mystery
plays she did not, at Chester or elsewhere, halt the moral
plays. In addition to such well-known plays as *Everyman*
and *The Three Estates*[1], there are many later ones, such as
*Liberality and Prodigality* and *All for Money*, written in the
last years of her reign. There are, also, echoes of the moral
plays in such works as *Dr Faustus* and *Volpone*, while
Shakespeare continually makes use of a knowledge of earlier
models, especially in *Measure for Measure*. In the provinces
the moral plays were the standard dramatic fare at the same
time as Londoners thought only of Marlowe, Shakespeare,
Jonson and their contemporaries. London has never been

[1] Both plays are obtainable in the present series. *Everyman* is to be found
in *Three Medieval Plays,* ed. John Allen.

typical of the rest of the country, and to recall this fact in the history of the drama will remove some of the misconceptions upon the absolute evolution and development of the English theatre from one type to another.

## The Mystery Plays

Before studying the Chester plays themselves it is necessary to assess the general importance of the English play cycles. They existed not only in the four northern cities which retain a cycle today but in over a hundred other towns and villages, and possibly in a great many more than we have any existing records of. The four major cycles hail from Chester, York, Wakefield and an unidentified northern city, possibly Lincoln, the home of the Hegge Plays or *Ludus Coventriae*. The original productions were all communal efforts handed out to different craft gilds by the corporation, which held the master-copy and insisted upon high standards of performance. From stage directions in Latin we may assume a learned producer controlling each unit. From the accounts we know that rehearsals were long and that a good deal of eating and drinking accompanied them. Craft elements were occasionally introduced, such as the axe, hatchet, hammer and hackstock of Noah and the weapons of the torturers at the crucifixion scene, and from this use it is not too much to say that these implements were spiritually dedicated in the eyes of the beholders. In the list of gilds occupied in the presentation of the Chester plays upon another page we can see how one corporation distributed the cycle to the crafts. Each company set forward at the appointed time in its wheeled stage, which had curtains and hangings around an upper platform and a lower hidden portion in which the properties were kept. After playing their sequence at one halt, the horses drew the carriages on throughout the day for the repetition of the scene at others. By allowing two or three plays to be given at the first point before sending the first pageant to the second point the organisers were able to ensure a

complete continuity, and it was in this way that most medieval
English plays were given, although the details of the wagon-
structure may have varied, and in some places, where the
size of the community did not warrant stopping places
*en route*, a scaffold was probably erected for one or more
performances in one central place.

Upon the normal principle, it will be noticed, there were
as many casts as there were plays, and a duplication of
important people was also inevitable. It is certain that the
ritual element in the plays attracted the spectators, who were,
in the mystical sense, also participants, and the sight of six
or seven different actors playing Christ in one day did not
cause any surprise. To add to the religious sense of participa-
tion, we should recall that the Pope offered indulgences to
all who behaved during the presentation of the plays in a
worthy manner.[1] It was the continuity of the Catholic
traditions that led Elizabeth I to ban the plays as exercises in
an unpopular religion.

It is not remembered today how great a variety of artistic
richness the plays offered their audiences. They were made
up of comedy, spectacle, pathos, activity, colour and music.
Centuries later, the composer Wagner was searching for a
general art-work (*gesamtkunstwerk*) in which all arts would
meet to subserve the purposes of opera. In the medieval
play-cycle there was exactly this inter-relation of the arts:
verse, solo and choral music with the tonal colours of different
musical instruments were to be heard while the visual
spectacle was unfolding. The Chester Drapers, though
pledged to the Creation play (some authorities attribute
this spectacle to the Mercers, however), attracted the eye
with satin, taffeta and damask upon their pageant, presumably
expended upon the décor and not the costume. No matter
how sophisticated the audience—it is absurd to believe that
only yokels attended—there was evidence of medieval

---

[1] To emphasise that the mystery cycle was a religious ritual before
anything else it should be noted that a superstition grew up that to look
upon the figure of the risen Christ insured the spectator against death
that year. This was not officially encouraged by the Church, however.

craftsmanship to be attractive to all. The play-cycle, indeed, offered in its texts a synthesis of the hopes and faith of medieval man and in its performance each year a perfect summary of his culture.

In the Middle Ages the art-styles of different countries mingled effortlessly together, while there were reflections of one art-form in the features of another. Paintings upon vellum, paintings upon walls, sculptures in marble, ivory and alabaster became a collective medieval art-form varying little from place to place and from decade to decade. As the art-historian, M. D. Whinney, writing of the twelfth century, remarks: " Valuable help was given by the older arts of the goldsmith and the illuminator to the rising techniques of the sculptor and the wall-painter." In the fourteenth century another art-form arrived to learn from all the others and to repay its debts most handsomely. In France, where the penetration is most obvious, there was, for instance, a greater variety in painted subjects offered after plays had enabled artists to have a more intense visual image of less important scenes. In the twelfth century they had depicted the primary feasts of the Church: later they could include the scenes between Jesus and Simon the Leper, or the woman taken in adultery (both in the present cycle), which have no date in the calendar but were nevertheless opportunities for new paintings. In the paintings of Jean Fouquet, Rogier van der Weyden, and Memlinc, the woodcuts of Dürer or Ghiberti's bronze doors in Florence we can see the influence of the theatre upon figure-groupings.

In Flanders there were many pictures depicting pageants as records of town-celebrations, and when the demand for purely religious drama died down all countries held pageants for state-occasions, often of the most elaborate secular-allegorical style. Leonardo da Vinci designed pageants in Milan, and Rubens often designed similar entertainments; Elizabeth I enjoyed secular pageants in her royal progresses, and so did most other monarchs. In 1549 Philip II of Spain, at an entertainment in Brussels, witnessed one which included an organ composed of cats! A cat with its tail tied to a key was imprisoned in each pipe, and as the musician struck the notes the required tail was pinched and catsong poured out. These secular departures were made possible by the popularity of the religious pageant and the changing taste of the Renaissance, yet they show the importance of the religious wheeled-theatre in the development of the history of sophisticated entertainment.

In England, unfortunately, the influence of the drama upon other art-forms appears to have been less rich. Stained glass windows and other images, studied by M. D. Anderson in *Drama and Imagery*, reveal various themes and techniques of the drama in churches where plays were known to have existed. There are two (and possibly more) English manuscript illuminations which show pageants looking like Punch and Judy shows, and there the contemporary depiction of the plays is virtually at an end. Only one other English art-form exists to provide reminders of them, and that is alabaster-carving. Men working in this medium learned to handle their pieces of alabaster with an increasing drama, and the centres of production of alabasters were in the north and in the region of the best plays. In some statues, for instance, we find a reflection of a dramatic convention known at Chester, the gilding of Christ's face, and in others we have the series of fifteen signs of the coming Antichrist, which were not known in any other cycles.

The drama also repaid its debts to other literary forms. In Chaucer, we can see how this was happening. The poet tells us that his Wife of Bath went to plays, and his Miller speaks in Pilate's voice and tells a tale full of drama. In it, Absolon, the parish-clerk, who had played Herod " on a scaffold high," and Nicholas, a student, outline a comic re-enaction of " Nowellis flude " certainly learned from a play. *The Miller's Tale* itself takes place upon three stage levels and is intensely dramatic: we have the carpenter asleep in his boat upon the roof, the wife with her lovers inside and outside the house, and at the end we have his fall to street-level when he believes that the flood has come and that he can launch his boat. I know of no better reflection or adaptation of the drama to other literary needs. More appropriately we may mention the relation between the plays and the medieval sermon. At Chester, for instance, there is a certain amount of theological exposition (a good deal of which has been cut in these pages), and this is explained when we remember that this is an early cycle, probably written by a churchman. Even unfamiliar figures like the midwives at Bethlehem and the damned souls on the Day of Judgement can be found in passages from sermons quoted in G. R. Owst's *Literature and the Pulpit in Medieval England*, which is an indispensable guide to the theology of the plays of Chester.

## THE CHESTER MYSTERY PLAYS

It was about 1375 that the Chester plays were first given, having possibly been written by Henry Francis at the far-sighted suggestion of one of the Mayors of the city. It is, unfortunately, not until the end of their performances in the reign of Elizabeth I that we have any printed documents to help explain their presentation. There were twenty-five pageants given upon the Monday, Tuesday and Wednesday after Pentecost: nine on the first day, nine on the second and seven on the third. We know that a gild whose play was in the first sequence might lend its wagon to another group, and that in Elizabethan times it cost about fifty shillings to mount the play each year.

In 1551 we read of the following payments:

| | |
|---|---|
| To Simeon | 3s. 6d. |
| To the Angel | 8d. |
| The little God | 12d. |
| Mary | 10d. |

Although the part is mute, a baby and not a doll was employed as Jesus and paid more than his mother, possibly because his face was gilded. In 1561 the details speak of rehearsals:

| Paid for the first rehearse | 6d. |
| Drink in barber's after the rehearse | 18d. |
| For beef against the general rehearse | 6s. 8d. |
| Three old cheeses | 4s. od. |

Further payments upon bread, beer, cheese, chickens, butter, beef and horse-bread abound in the pages of the accounts, and show us actors not satisfied with a simple supper. One actor is given as much as 3s. 7d. either because he was a professional player, or a cleric, or else a star. In 1574 a star actor engaged by the Cooper's company was rather temperamental, and we read:

Spent on Thomas Marler to get him to play    2d.

In their last fifty years the cycle's performances became sporadic (except during the short reign of Mary), for voices of dissent were being heard. In 1571 the performance took place " though many of the city were sore against the setting forth." In 1574 anti-Popery assumed greater proportions, and the last full version was played either in 1575 or 1576, though some pageants set out in 1577. Thereafter nothing was heard of them. Games and the fairground swallowed up the mysteries, and of the new entertainments we have some inkling in Jonson's *Bartholomew Fair*. In 1595 the first professional players arrived in Chester, probably bringing Morality drama, and thereafter the townspeople became onlookers and not participants and this was not entirely to their taste. They were probably reluctant to lose the traditional holiday spectacle, and it was only government action that brought an end to the old plays. We recall that the Elizabethan order was asserted with the assistance of spies and secret police up and down the country: a perfect acceptance of royal commands there emphatically was not in the northern towns that lost their plays when the prompt-copies were called in for scrutiny and not returned.

Fortunately for us a text was left, and between 1591 and 1607 no less than five manuscript copies of the cycle were commissioned by men with antiquarian interests. To them we remain permanently indebted, and from their texts we have the one printed version in the original spelling in the series of the Early English Text Society, which is the basis of the present adaptation.

The Chester Plays are preceded by the Banns, which were read in the city before the plays were given as a summons to the audience and as a programme giving the list of the plays and gilds employed in verse. The following is the original list of the complete cycle:

|     |                                              |                                        |
| --- | -------------------------------------------- | -------------------------------------- |
| 1.  | *The Fall of Lucifer*                        | The Tanners                            |
| 2.  | *The Creation*                               | The Drapers                            |
| 3.  | *The Deluge*                                 | The Waterleaders and Drawers in the Dee |
| 4.  | *Abraham, Melchisedech and Lot* (*The Sacrifice of Isaac*) | The Barbers              |
| 5.  | *\*Balaam and Balak*                         | The Cappers                            |
| 6.  | *The Nativity*                               | The Wrights                            |
| 7.  | *The Adoration of the Shepherds*             | The Painters and Glaziers              |
| 8.  | *The Adoration of the Magi*                  | The Vintners                           |
| 9.  | *The Magi's Oblation*                        | The Mercers                            |
| 10. | *The Slaying of the Innocents*               | The Goldsmiths                         |
| 11. | *\*The Purification*                         | The Blacksmiths                        |
| 12. | *The Temptation of Christ*                   | The Butchers                           |
| 13. | *Christ, The Adultress, Chelidonus and Lazarus* | The Glovers                         |
| 14. | *Christ's Visit to Simon the Leper*          | The Corvisars                          |
| 15. | *Christ's Betrayal*                          | The Bakers                             |
| 16. | *Christ's Passion*                           | The Bowyers, Fletchers and Ironmongers |
| 17. | *\*Christ's Descent into Hell*               | The Cooks and Innkeepers               |
| 18. | *Christ's Resurrection*                      | The Skinners                           |
| 19. | *\*Christ appears to two Disciples*          | The Saddlers                           |
| 20. | *Christ's Ascension*                         | The Tailors                            |
| 21. | *\*The Sending of the Holy Ghost*            | The Fishmongers                        |
| 22. | *\*The Prophets and Antichrist*              | The Clothiers and Shearmen             |
| 23. | *The Coming of Antichrist*                   | The Dyers                              |
| 24. | *The Last Judgement*                         | The Websters                           |

There was also an additional play completely lost:

|     |                         |                                |
| --- | ----------------------- | ------------------------------ |
| 25. | *Our Lady's Assumption* | The Worshipful Wives of Chester |

\* Omitted in the present version.

## This Version

Our ancestors enjoyed three days for the performance of their plays and not a three-hour maximum. They also had an immense potential cast. We are not well supplied in either way, and a modern version must omit whole plays, shorten episodes and reduce where possible the number of small-part players as well as the length of some leisurely speeches. All this has been done in the present version, though it is hoped that enough remains to give an idea of the extent of the whole. Cutting by individual producers will still be necessary, but for readers a greater leisure may be assumed. The language is generally such as can be understood from the stage, and where a few medieval expressions have been retained (" I wis," " by my fay," etc.) they are familiar to all who have knowledge of Elizabethan plays, and it is largely because rhyming demanded their retention. The arranger is aware that the rhyming is now not perfect, but this is more frequently the case in the original text. The division into five parts is not found in the original.

## Part I

From the five Old Testament plays in the cycle one is here missing, that of Balaam and Balak. The function of the scenes after the Creation was largely theological in that they were chosen with the express purpose of showing a relation between events in the Old and New Testaments, how one prefigured the other. Noah, Abraham and Isaac are excellent instances of the play as a commentary on the structure of the Bible as well as a dramatisation. The pattern on which the cycle was shaped will be seen in the chart on p. xxii.

In the Creation we have superb alliterative lines from God, different in form from the stanza-pattern of most of the subsequent plays. Their firm rhythms must be given the fullest weight by the speaker. Afterwards, the most fascinating scene here is the Deluge with its boatbuilding and the description of a world teeming with animals. Upon the human plane we have the character of Mrs. Noah who first gave rise to much of the literary satire upon her sex in the Middle Ages, although in other cycles she is more tempestuous than here. The closing description of the rainbow rises to unexpected poetic heights, especially here:

> Where clouds in the skies have been
> That new bow shall be seen
> In token that my wrath and spleen
> Never again shall wreaked be.
>
> The string is turned towards you
> And towards me is bent the bow
> That such weather shall never show,
> And this promise I thee.

The poignancy of Abraham and Isaac is intended as a lesson in filial obedience just as the reluctance of Mrs. Noah was a dramatic example of the need for marital obedience. It is, however, a great deal more, in that it prefigures Christ's sacrifice. As the tension of this scene mounts the author employs a most powerful and almost Shakespearean command of familiar detail:

> My dear father, I you pray,
> Let me take my clothes away.
> Fear shedding blood on them today
> At my last ending.

## PART II

The Nativity sequences have the incident of Joseph and the midwives, for which we look in vain in the Bible, drawn from the apocryphal book, the *Protevangelion* of St James the Less. The beauty of the Nativity is in no whit impaired by the gormandising of the shepherds for this adds a local and earthy humour as a perfect foil to the mystical and universal events that follow, and it is also cited as proof that the plays were written before the Black Death removed many items from the menu. In compensation for it the Chester shepherds become preachers after visiting Christ, and here we have one example of the greater didacticism of the present cycle compared with the others. The better-known play from the Towneley Cycle concerning Mak the sheep-stealer is a finer play, but its greater secularisation is hard to integrate into the mystery of the stable for a modern mind.

The Magi's plays are dominated by Herod, who shows the boldness demanded of him. His farcical death, duplicated in Play 16, is the only conceivable end for such brazenness, and a piece of dramatic satire which may have had influence upon the satirical plays of Marlowe or Jonson. As a girl of sixteen Mary presides over the Nativity without a great assertion of character, but assisted by an old and bewildered Joseph, a sympathetic human person amazed at the unexpected events in his family. The picture thus created is not biblical, but it is the traditional presentation of Joseph in medieval drama.

## PART III

The plays concerning the ministry of Jesus are condensed here from three in the original to two, to a moment of rest while the different threads of the Betrayal are woven. The mind of Judas in this scene is an absorbing study and the reactions of the crowd are skilfully handled as they prepare their case against the Saviour. It is a part of the cycle in which actions come faster than before and the tempo does not flag until the Crucifixion is past.

The final moment before the Passion, the Last Supper, shows again purely human doubts and conflicts in face of historic events. One symbolic fact should be kept in mind here: Christ's sacrifice is the culmination of those already acted, from Noah and Abraham. The upper room should be identified with the raised level of the stage employed for those sacrifices to establish this theological point. We notice, too, the abstraction of Christ from his own Passion and his indulgence towards Malchus and even Judas who was involuntarily involved in this paradoxically happy tragedy.

## PART IV

The Passion itself was originally the longest of the plays and a pageant shared by three gilds. The first section shows a sympathetic Pilate, devoted to justice and logic, familiar perhaps to the reader of Bacon's Essays. Washing his hands in public is a magnificent gesture, and his tone throughout is far removed from melodramatic villainy: Annas and Caiaphas are more truly villainous. Since the physical torture is great a number of the speeches of derision and lamentation have been cut, but our attention is drawn to the return of the sorrowful mother under the Cross. She gives rise to a calmer emotional tone which the closing stages of so intense a drama demands. It was a grim irony of the bowyers, fletchers and stringers to club together with iron-mongers to give this pageant, and the text gives them opportunities to exert their crafts in the violence of the action. As Christ dies there is a pause: a storm can be imagined here or strident music over which the last speech is delivered as the body is taken down from the cross.

In the scene of the Resurrection the dominant emotions are the fear of the warriors and deep repentance: we are back again with the human beings, and the Chester poet has handled the verse with great beauty.

The Ascension is the last fully dramatic play in the cycle; what is to come is more and more verbal. The actual ascent is accompanied by other souls released from Hell in a scene omitted here, and with it we leave the gospel narrative. The action falls slowly off as the cycle shades more and more into theological disquisition.

## PART V

There remain two plays of the future, like an epilogue. It opens with a speech from the Expositor which could in no way be omitted because of its importance in the structure of the whole cycle, although the rest of the play, full of long prophecies is not missed. This long speech is a perfect counterbalance to the Creation and Deluge plays. With it we have the following structural scheme for the whole cycle:

1. Chaos—Creation—Deluge (chaos repeated)—Christ's birth.
2. Christ's death—Antichrist—Chaos repeated—Judgement Day.

Antichrist himself is a creature of extreme audacity: he is best viewed as an unexpected visitor whose actions will astonish an audience and who provides employment for the devil who has been off duty for a long time. Though Antichrist is often mentioned in works of theology he appeared in no other English play.

The Judgement is highly selective here, though it is as well to imagine other souls for the judgement. The scene points out its lesson of charity towards the repentant sinner again, and reminds us that sinners are not happy on earth in their sins, and that they may yet attain to divine forgiveness. The final moment is reserved for the devils with a short and appropriate epilogue from the four evangelists who provided the sources of most of the plays.

## FURTHER READING

A great deal has been written upon the subject of the medieval drama though most of it is intended for the specialist. The following books may be recommended:

E. K. CHAMBERS, *The Medieval Stage* (2 vols. O.U.P.).

HARDIN CRAIG, *English Religious Drama* (O.U.P.).

V. A. KOLVE, *The Play Called Corpus Christi* (Stanford Univ. Press).

F. M. SALTER, *Medieval Drama in Chester* (Toronto Univ. Press).

GLYNNE WICKHAM, *Early English Stages: Vol. I* (Routledge).

ROSEMARY WOOLF, *The English Mystery Plays* (Routledge).

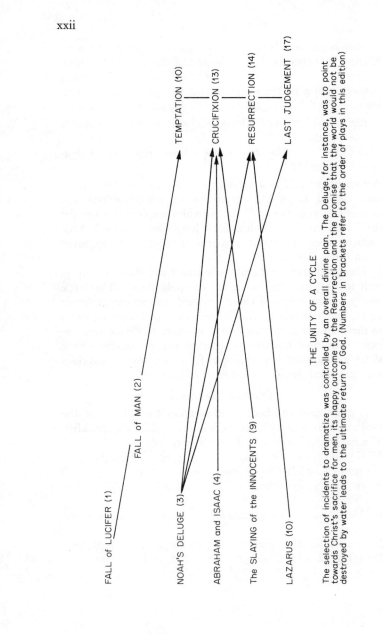

THE UNITY OF A CYCLE

The selection of incidents to dramatize was controlled by an overall divine plan. The Deluge, for instance, was to point towards Christ's sacrifice for men, its happy outcome to the Resurrection and the promise that the world would not be destroyed by water leads to the ultimate return of God. (Numbers in brackets refer to the order of plays in this edition)

# CHARACTERS

### THE FALL OF LUCIFER

| | | |
|---|---|---|
| God the Father | Lucifer | Lightborne |
| Angels | Archangels | Virtues |
| Cherubim | Seraphim | Dominations |
| Principalities | Thrones | Potentates |

### THE CREATION OF MAN

| | | |
|---|---|---|
| God the Father | Adam & Eve | The Devil |

### NOAH'S DELUGE

| | | |
|---|---|---|
| God the Father | Noah | Mother Noah |
| Sem & his Wife | Ham & his Wife | Japhet & his Wife |

### ABRAHAM AND ISAAC

| | | |
|---|---|---|
| God the Father | Abraham & Isaac | An Angel |

### THE NATIVITY

| | | |
|---|---|---|
| Archangel Gabriel | Mary | Tebell & Salome |
| Joseph | An Angel | (Midwives) |

### THE ADORATION OF THE SHEPHERDS

| | | |
|---|---|---|
| Three Shepherds | An Angel | Mary & Joseph |

### THE ADORATION OF THE MAGI

| | | |
|---|---|---|
| Three Kings | An Angel | Herod |
| A Messenger | A Doctor | |

### THE MAGI'S OBLATION

| | | |
|---|---|---|
| Three Kings | An Angel | Mary & Joseph |

### THE SLAYING OF THE INNOCENTS

| | | |
|---|---|---|
| Herod | Preco | An Angel |
| Two Soldiers | Mary | Joseph |
| The Devil | Two Women | Women & Children |

### THE TEMPTATION

| | | |
|---|---|---|
| Satan | Jesus | Two Jews |
| Woman | Martha & Mary | Lazarus |

I

## SIMON THE LEPER

| | | |
|---|---|---|
| Jesus | Peter | Philip |
| Simon | Lazarus | Martha |
| Mary Magdalene | Judas | Pharisees |
| Caiaphas | Merchants | |

## THE BETRAYAL OF CHRIST

| | | |
|---|---|---|
| Jesus | Peter | John |
| A Servant | Lord of the House | Andrew |
| James | Judas | Thomas |
| Philip | Malchus | Soldiers |
| Jews | Other Disciples | |

## CHRIST'S PASSION

| | | |
|---|---|---|
| Annas | Caiaphas | Jesus |
| Pilate | John | Mary |
| Simon of Cyrene | Jews | Joseph of Arimathæa |

## CHRIST'S RESURRECTION

| | | |
|---|---|---|
| Caiaphas | Pilate | Annas |
| Three Soldiers | Jesus | Mary Magdalene |
| Mary Jacobi | Mary Salome | Two Angels |
| Peter | | |

## CHRIST'S ASCENSION

| | | |
|---|---|---|
| Jesus | Peter | Andrew |
| John | James | Angels |

## ANTICHRIST

| | | |
|---|---|---|
| Expositor | Antichrist | Two Kings |
| Two Dead Men | Enoch | Elias |
| Two Devils | Archangel Michael | |

## THE LAST JUDGEMENT

| | | |
|---|---|---|
| God the Father | Angels | Two Popes |
| Two Emperors | Two Queens | Jesus |
| Devils | Four Evangelists | The Damned and Saved |

# PART I

GOD: I am Alpha and Omega,
  Foremost and noblest.
  Being my will it should be so,
  It is, it was and shall be thus.

  I am great and gracious God that never had any beginning;
  The whole substance of begetting lies in my essence.
  I am the root of the Trinity that shall never split;
  Peerless Patron imperial and Father of wisdom.
  My trumpets sound beatitudes; my behests bring all bliss;
  Both visible and invisible, all is my working;
  As God, great and glorious, all lies in my laws.

  For all might of majesty is magnified in Me,
  Prince principal, proved by my perpetual providence,
  I was never but one and ever One in Three
  Set in steadfast truth within my heavenly wisdom.
  Three Spirits on a throne, truly a trinity,
  Take root in my Godhead and exaltation from my excellence;
  The might of my making is all marked in me,
  Formed by my divine experience under my diadem.

  Now since I am thus solemn and set in isolation
  A mighty palace of bliss will I build, a heaven without end,
  And make a comely circle through my comely creation:
  Nine orders of Angels shall attend me here.
  Do your bidding and have no doubts under my domination
  But sit in celestial safety where all solace is seen,
  Where all forms in my Empire render praise to my love
  And by my highest might happiness shall be without
    ending.

3

LUCIFER: Lord, through thy grace and might thou hast us
  wrought,
  Nine orders of Angels here as you may see:
  Cherubim and Seraphim, through your thought,
  Thrones and Dominations in bliss to be

  With Principalities, that order bright,
  And Potentates in blissful height
  And Virtues through thy great might,
  Angels and Archangels beside.

  Nine orders here there truly be
  That you have made full bright;
  In thy bliss they rightly be
  And I principal lord here in thy sight.

GOD: Now, Lucifer and Lightborne, look well you attend.
  The blessing of my benignity I give my first works:
  For neither craft nor cunning can ever comprehend
  Or exalt you to the exultation of high excellence.
  Look that you do all things wisely while I wend away.
  The world that is both void and vain I form in this shape
  With a deep, dark dungeon that shall have no ending.
  These works are now done by my divine plan.

ANGELS: We thank thee, Lord in sovereignty
  That us hath made so clean and clear,
  Ever in this bliss to abide with Thee.
  Grant us thy grace to live ever here.

ARCHANGELS: Here to abide God grant us grace
  To please this Prince without a peer;
  Him now to thank with great solace
  A song now let us sing together.          (*They sing*)

GOD: Now since I have formed you so fair
  And exalted you so excellent,

And here I set you next my Chair,
My love for you is so fervent,
Look lest you fall into despair;
Touch not my throne without assent
Or all your beauty I shall impair
And pride bring ruin to all your intent.

LUCIFER: Nay, Lord, that shall we never indeed;
For nothing shall trespass 'gainst Thee
The great Godhead shall we all dread
And never exalt ourselves so free.
Thou hast made us with might and main
In Thy bliss evermore to bide and be,
To everlasting our life to lead
And bearer of light thou hast made me.

LIGHTBORNE: And I am made of that same mould
To offer all love to our Creator
That has made us gayer than gold
In his grace ever here to endure.

GOD: I now forbid that you ever should
Do aught but keep in this stature.
This same covenant I charge you hold
In fear of my heaven's forfeiture.

For I must wend a path to trace
To set this bliss in every tower.
Each one of you will keep his place
And Lucifer, I make thee governor.

Now I charge thee all, in grace,
That you recall my order.
Behold the beams of my bright face
Which ever was, and shall endure.

This be your joy in every case
Aye to behold your creator;
No other is like me through all space
Nor shall be like unto my figure.

Now shall I leave for another place
To be the Angels' comforter;
I shall return in a short space
Such is my will, in this same hour.                              (*Exit*)

LUCIFER: Ha! am I not wondrous bright
　　Among you all shining so clear?
　　Of all Heaven I bear the light
　　Though God himself were still here.

　　If on this throne I only were
　　Then I should be as wise as he.
　　What say you, angels, do you hear?
　　Some comfort soon grant all to me.

VIRTUES: We will not assent unto your pride,
　　Nor in hearts harbour such a thought,
　　Only our Lord shall be our guide
　　To keep us in mind of what he hath wrought.

CHERUBIM: Our Lord commanded all of us here
　　To keep his commands, the great and the less,
　　Therefore we warn thee, Lucifer,
　　Thy pride will turn to distress.

LUCIFER: Distress! I command you now to cease
　　And see the beauty I bear;
　　All heaven shines through me alone
　　God himself shines never so clear.

DOMINATIONS: Of all Angels you bear the prize
　　And most beauty to you does befall.
　　My counsel to you is, be wise
　　Lest you like a slave lie in thrall.

PRINCIPALITIES: If to such slavery yourself you bring
　　Then you shall know a wicked fall.
　　So shall all your new offspring;
　　Away with you shall they all.

SERAPHIM: Our brethren's counsel is good to hear,
   To you we say, Lucifer and Lightborne,
   Beware of the power of this Chair
   Lest God shall fiercely you spurn.

LIGHTBORNE: In faith, brother, yet you shall
   Sit in this throne both clean and clear.
   For you shall be as wise withal
   As God Himself, if He were here.

   Therefore set yourself here,
   That all heaven may you behold.
   The brightness of your body fair
   Is brighter than God's a thousandfold.

LUCIFER: Here will I sit now in his stead,
   To exalt myself, not bend the knee;
   Behold my body, my hands and head,
   The might of God is marked in me.
   All Angels, turn to me, instead
   For here your sovereign now you see,
   I am your Comfort, Lord and head,
   In the gay might of majesty.

LIGHTBORNE: And I stand next in the same degree,
   By right of the same experience;
   If I should only sit here by thee,
   All heaven should do me reverence.
   All orders now come from thee and from me,
   So hast thou placed us by thy eloquence.
   If here were only the Trinity
   We should surpass Him in intelligence.

DOMINATIONS: Alas! why make you this great offence?
   You Lucifer and Lightborne, to both I say:
   Our sovereign Lord will have you hence
   If he finds you in this array.

Go to your places or run from hence
You have begun a perilous play
And shall soon know the consequence;
This dance will bring you a woeful way.

LUCIFER: I tell you all, do me reverence,
For I am full of heavenly grace.
If God comes back, I will not from thence,
But sit still here before his face.          (*He sits on throne*)

GOD: Say, what array do I find here?
Who is your prince and principal?     (*They shake and tremble*)
I made thee, O Angel Lucifer,
And here thou wouldst be lord over all!
Therefore I charge you with order clear
That fast from this place you now shall fall;
Now, at once, I shall change your cheer
And for foul pride to hell now you shall.

Lucifer, who set thee here, when I must go?
How have I given offence to thee?
I made thee my friend, now be my foe.
Among all the angels there was none, as you know,
That sat so closely to my Majesty.
I charge you fall till I say " No "
In the pit of hell evermore to be.          (*They fall into the pit*)

DEVIL LUCIFER: Alas! that ever we were wrought
That we should come to such a place!
We lived in joy, now we are nought.
Alas, we have all lost our hopes of grace!

DEVIL LIGHTBORNE: Now see whither thou hast us brought
To a dungeon, small path to trace.
All this sorrow 'tis thou hast sought,
The Devil speed thy stinking face!

LUCIFER: My face, false traitor, off you fare!
    Thou hast brought us to this woeful array.
    I am encumbered, cankered, racked with care,
    Sunk deep in sorrow; what can I say?

LIGHTBORNE: Thou hast brought us all this wicked way
    With all thy might and pride,
    Away from bliss that would last for aye
    In sorrow ever more here to abide.

LUCIFER: Your plan it was as well as mine,
    Behind that pride we both did show,
    Now both lie here in hell to pine
    Until the trumpets of the day of doom shall blow.

LIGHTBORNE: Then we shall not care for woe
    But lie here like two fiends black.
    Alas, we had to forfeit so
    The Lord's love that did us make.

LUCIFER: And therefore I shall for his sake
    Show mankind great envy
    As soon as He can him make
    I shall him at once destroy.

    Some of my charge shall it be
    To make mankind all to do amiss.
    Ruffian, my friend, fair and free,
    Look that you keep man from bliss.

    Since I and my fellows fell down for aye
    God will ordain mankind again
    To bliss with the great array
    And we evermore in hell pain.

LIGHTBORNE: Out! Harrow! where is our might
    That we once were wont to show,
    When we in heaven bore such great light
    Though now in hell full low?

LUCIFER: Alas! for all our woe and wickedness!
   I am bound so fast in this plight and cheer,
   And never away from hence may pass
   But lie in hell with all for ever still.          (*Exeunt*)

GOD: Ay! wicked pride shall ever work thee woe
   My joy thou hast made amiss.
   I may well suffer: my will is not so
   That they should part thus from my bliss.
   Ah pride, why hast thou not burst in two?
   Why did they that? Why did they this?
   Behold, my Angels: pride is your foe,
   All sorrow shall show wherever it is.

   And though they have broken my Commandment
   I rue it full sore and sufferingly;
   Nevertheless I will have mine intent;
   What first I thought shall still come to be.
   Myself and the Trinity agrees with consent
   A solemn matter now to try.
   A full fair image shall soon hence be sent
   That its same seed shall multiply.

   In my blessing here I begin
   The first thing in my glory and right:
   Lightness and darkness? I bid both be seen,
   The night in its dark, the day in its light.

   As I have made all things of nought,
   After my will and my wishing,
   My first day now have I wrought,
   I give it here fully my blessing.

**END OF FIRST PLAY**

### 2.   The Creation of Man: Adam and Eve

GOD: Now heaven earth is made through me,
The voidness of earth is all I can see,

At my bidding now made be light.
Light is good, I see in my sight;
Divided shall be through my might
The light from the star's ray.

Light day I will have called for aye,
And stars night, as I say;
Thus morn and even the first day
Is made full and without delay.

Now will I make the firmament
In the midst of the waters to be sent,
To act as it were a divider
To part the waters for ever.

Above the welkin, and beneath also,
And into heaven it shall go.
Thus evening is come and then the morrow
Of the second day.

Now will I the waters where they do run
Under Heaven and under the sun
That they should all gather themselves into one
And dryness soon shall show.

That dryness earth men shall call,
The gatherings of the waters all,
Seas is the name for them all,
Thereby men shall them know.

I will on earth that herbs shall spring
Each one in its kind its seed giving,
Trees many fruits into light shall bring
And after their kind, each one.

The seed of each for aye shall be
Within the fruit of each tree,
Thus morn and even of days three
Are both come and gone.

Now will I make through my might
Lightening in the welkin bright
To mark the day from the night
And lighten the earth and sea.

Great lights I will make two;
The sun and the moon also,
The sun shall shine all day through,
The moon for night to be.

I will make on the firmament
Stars also, through mine intent
The earth to lighten they shall be lent
To man to know, thereby,

Courses of planets, with nothing amiss.
Now I see this work is all good, I wis,
Thus morning and even, both made is
Of the full fourth day.

Now will I in waters fish forth bring,
Fowls in the firmament be flying,
Great whales in the sea swimming
All made from my thought.

Beasts, fowls, stone and tree,
These works are good, that I can see,
Therefore to bless all gladdens me
These works that I have wrought.

All beasts, I bid you multiply
In earth and water, by and by
And fowls in the air to fly
The earth to fill.

Thus morn and even through my might
Of the fifth day and the night
Is made and ended well aright
All at mine own will.

Now on earth will I bring anon
All kinds of beasts, every one
That creep, fly or else move on,
Each one in his kind.

Now this is done at my bidding:
Beasts going, flying, creeping,
And all my works to my liking
Fully now I find.

Now Heaven and earth are made express,
Make we man to our likeness:
Fish, fowl, beasts, greater and less
To master shall he have the right.

In our shape now make I thee,
Man and woman I will there be,
Grow and multiply also shall ye
And fulfil earth with might.

Now this is done, I see aright
And all things made through my might
The sixth day now, here in my sight
Is made all of the best.

Heaven and earth is wrought with peace
And all that needs to be therein;
Tomorrow the seventh day, I will cease
And from my work take rest.

But now this man that I have made
With spirit of life fully arrayed,
Rise up, Adam, rise, be not afraid,
A man full of soul and life.

And come with me to Paradise
A place packed with dainty device,
It is good that thou shouldst be wise
Bring not thyself into strife.

Here Adam I give thee this place
Thee to comfort and to solace;
Keep to it, and thy whole race,
And do as I thee say.          (*Takes* ADAM *to Paradise*)

Of all the trees that be herein
Shalt thou eat and nothing sin,
But of this tree for good therein
Thou shalt eat in no way.

If thou eatest of this tree,
Death will come, believe thou me,
Therefore this fruit, I tell thee, flee
And be thou not so bold.

Beasts and fowls that thou may see
To thee obedient shall ever be.
What name they be given by thee
That name they shall ever hold.

(GOD *causes him to lie down*)

It is not good man alone to be
Help for him now make we;
But to cause sleep behoveth me
Anon in this man here.                    (ADAM *sleeps*)

Asleep thou art now, well I see;
Therefore a bone I take of thee,
And flesh also with heart free
To make thee a mate.

ADAM: O Lord, where have I so long been?
For since I slept much have I seen
That all have truly wonders been
Hereafter to be known.

GOD: Hear, Adam, rise and wake.
Behold a wife made for thy sake,
And her to thee now shalt thou take
And name her as thine own.                (ADAM *rises*)

ADAM: I see well, Lord, through thy grace,
Bone of my bone in her I trace
And flesh of my flesh I see in her face,
Of my shape through thy word.

Therefore shall she be called, I wis,
Woman, and nothing amiss
For out of man she taken is
And to man is she bound.

Therefore man shall kindly forsake
Father and mother a wife him to take,
Two in one flesh, as Thou canst make
Each other to make glad.           (*They stand together*)

DEVIL: Out, out! what sorrow is this?
That I have lost so much bliss.
For once I think I did amiss
Out of heaven I fell.

The brightest angels I was ere this
That ever was or yet is,
But pride cast me down, I wis,
From heaven right down to hell.

Spiritual paradise was I in
But thence I fell through my sin;
Of earthly paradise now, as I have seen
A man is given mastery.

Should such a caitiff, made of clay,
Have such bliss? No, by this day.
For I shall teach his wife a play
If I may have a while.

Her to deceive I hope I may
And through her bring both away
For she will do whatever I say.
Her I hope to beguile.

Disguise me I will that I can see
And offer her of that tree
So shall they both for their disloyalty
Be banished forever from bliss.

A manner of an adder is in this place
With wings like a bird around her to lace,
Feet like an adder, but a maiden's face;
Her form I will take.


And of that tree of Paradise
Shall she eat through my subtle advice
For women are caught with a dainty device
And she shall not deny,


And eat of it she will full greedily.
They both shall fare as did I,
Be banished both from this valley
With their offspring for aye.


Woman, why was God so nice
To bid desert your dainty device
And of each tree of paradise
To forsake the meat?


EVE: Nay, of the fruit of each tree
For to eat good leave have we,
Save the fruit of one we must flee
And of it we must not eat.


This tree here in midst now is
If we eat of it we do amiss.
God said we should die, I wis,
If we touch that tree.


DEVIL: Woman, I say: leave not this.
It can lose you no bliss
Nor no joy that is His
But be as wise as He.

Take of this fruit and taste this day.
It is good food, I will lay,
And if thou find'st that thou must pay
Say that I am all false.

Eat thou one apple and no more
And you shall know both weal and woe,
And be like Gods wherever you go,
Thou and thy husband also.

EVE: Ah, lord, this tree is fair and bright
Green and seemly in my sight,
The fruit sweet and full of might
That gods it can us make.

An apple of it I will eat,
To see the taste of its fine meat
And my husband I will meet
To take a morsel too.

Adam, husband; my life so dear,
Eat some of this apple here;
It is sweet, now have no fear,
You will enjoy it without mistake.                (ADAM *eats*)

ADAM: That is true, Eve, I have no fear;
The fruit is sweet and fair, my dear.
Therefore I will do thy prayer
And one morsel will I take.

Out! alas! what ails me?
I am naked, that well I see.
Woman, cursed must thou be,
Away we shall be sent.

I know not for shame whether to flee
For this fruit was forbidden me.
Now have I broken, through word from thee,
My Lord's commandment.

EVE: Alas! this Adder! Alas! o fie!
  Take her counsel? Why did I?
  Naked we are, and of our thigh
  And human shape ashamed.

ADAM: Yes, truly I said in prophecy
  When thou wast taken out of my body
  Man's woe thou wouldst be surely,
  And therefore wast thou named.

EVE: Adam, husband, I now shall take
  These fig-leaves for shame's sake
  And to our members a covering make
  Both for thee and me.          *(Dons fig-leaves)*

ADAM: Therewith my members I will hide
  And under this tree I now must bide
  For surely, when God comes here beside
  Out of this place go we.

GOD: Adam, Adam. Where art thou?

ADAM: Ah! Lord, I heard thy voice right now.
  I am naked, that I vow.
  Therefore do I hide me.

GOD: Who told thee, Adam, thou naked was,
  Save only thine own trespass,
  That of that tree thou eaten has
  Though I forbade thee?

ADAM: Lord, this woman that is here,
That thou gavest me to be my dear,
She gave me part: and at her prayer
Some of it I did eat.

GOD: Woman, why hast thou done so?

EVE: This adder, Lord, she was my foe,
Truly she deceived me so
And made me eat that meat.

GOD: Adder, for that thou has done this harm
Among all beasts on earth that swarm
I curse thee now with my right arm
For this woman's sake.

Upon thy belly thou shalt go,
And eat the earth and to and fro,
And enmity betwixt ye two
Henceforth I shall make.

Betwixt they seed and hers also
I shall excite sorrow and woe;
To crush thy head and be thy foe
She shall have mastery aye.

No beast on earth, I now do say,
Shall man so hate all his day.
Thou shalt be trodden into the clay
For thy misdeed here today.          (*Serpent crawls away*)

And, woman, I warn thee truly,
Thy mischief I shall multiply,
With penance, sorrow and great annoy
Thy children shalt thou bear.

And since thou hast done so today
The man shalt master thee alway
And under his power thou shalt be aye
Thee to drive into care.


And man, also, I say to thee,
For thou hast not done after me,
Thy wife's counsel ever to flee
For doing so her bidding


To eat the fruit of this tree,
Wearied in thy work on the earth thou shalt be
And in great labour behoveth thee
On earth to get thy living.


When on earth thou hast worked thy space
Fruit shall not grow in any place
But briars and thorns for thy trespass
To thee on the earth shall spring.


Herbs and roots shalt thou eat
And for thy sustenance sorely sweat
With great effort to win thy meat
Nothing to thy liking.


ADAM: Alas! to languish now am I left
How suddenly of all bereft.
I have lost all of God's gift
And can never find another.


My gluttonous wife has been my foe
And the devil's envy hit me also.
These two together well may go
Like sister and brother.

GOD: Now shall you go from this country:
    Covered you now must be.
    Dead beasts' skins, it seems to me
    Were best for you to bear.

    For mortal both, now are ye,
    And death in no way shall you flee;
    Dead skins are best for your degree
    And such now shall ye wear.     (GOD *gives them skins*)

    Now lest thou covetest kindness more
    And do as thou hast done before,
    And eat of this fruit to live evermore
    Here thou must not be.

    There to the earth thou must go yon,
    With travail to lead thy life thereon
    For there is no course but now to be gone.
    Go forth and take Eve with thee.
        (GOD *drives them out of Paradise*)

### END OF SECOND PLAY

### 3. NOAH'S DELUGE

GOD: I, God, that all the world have wrought:
    Heaven and earth and all from naught,
    I see my people in deed and thought
    Are set foully in sin.

    My joy cannot linger in man
    That, through sin, lies under my ban.
    But wait six score years more I can
    To leave their old sin.

Man that I made I will destroy,
Beast, worm and fowl all die,
For on earth all me deny,
Those folk that dwell thereon.

It harms me so hurtfully,
That malice should multiply.
Sore it pains me inwardly,
That ever I made man.

Therefore, Noah, my servant free,
That righteous man art as I can see,
A ship soon thou shalt make thee
Of trees dry and light.

Little chambers therein thou shalt make
And binding ropes also thou take.
Cease not with cord and with stake
To make fast with all thy might.

Three hundred cubits shall it be long
And Fifty in breadth to make it strong,
Fifty more high, so be ye not wrong
And measure it about.

One window make with thy might
One cubit in breadth and height.
In the side a door fit thou right
For to come in and out.

Eating places make thou also,
High roofed chambers, one or two,
For with water I mean to flow
Over that man I did make.

Destroyed all the world shall be
Save thou, thy wife and sons three,
And all their wives also with thee
Shall be saved for thy sake.

NOAH: Ah, lord, I thank thee loud and still
That to me art in good will,
And spare me and my home not spill
As here now I find.

Thy bidding, Lord, I shall fulfil,
And never shall grieve or do ill
That such grace shows your high will
Among all mankind.

Have done, you men and women all,
Help in whatever may now befall
To work this ship, build chamber and hall
As God has bidden us do.

SEM: Father, here I am come from the town
An axe I have here, by my crown.
I lay we shall not soon drown.
Let us go to.

HAM: I have a hatchet wondrous keen,
To bite well as may be seen,
One better ground, sure I ween,
Is not in this town.

JAPHET: And I can make such a pin
And with this hammer knock it in.
Go and work without more din
Then we shall not drown.

MOTHER NOAH: And we shall bring timber to you.
   There is nothing else that we can do
   For women are weak yet they will help too
   In this great travail.

SEM'S WIFE: Here is a good hackstock:
   On this you may hew and knock.
   There shall none be idle in all this flock
   And no one shall fail.

HAM'S WIFE: And I will go and heat some pitch
   To daub and fill up every niche.
   Anointed it must be in every stitch,
   Board, tree and pin.

JAPHET'S WIFE: And I will gather woodchips here
   To make a fire for you, for fear
   There is no meal done here
   Against your coming in.

NOAH: Now in the name of God I will begin
   To make the ship we shall go in
   That we may all be ready to swim
   At the coming of the flood.

   These boards I join here together
   To keep us safe in the wet weather
   That we may row hither and thither
   And be safe from the flood.

   Of this tree will I make the mast
   Tied up with cables that will last
   With a sail yard for every sharp blast
   And whatever God send.

With topsail and bowsprit
With cords and ropes I have what is fit
To sail forth when it grows wet.
This ship is at an end.

Wife, in this castle we shall be kept.
When my children and you in have leapt.

MOTHER NOAH: In faith, Noah, I would sooner you slept
Than all this stupid fussing.
I will not do as you have said.

NOAH: Good wife, do as I thee bid.

MOTHER NOAH: By Christ! not till I see more need
Though you stand all day here staring.

NOAH: Lord, all women are crabbed.  Aye!
And never are meek, that I will say.
This is well seen on earth this day
Which witness you, each one

Good wife, let be all this jeer
That thou makest standing here,
For all will think you are master
And so thou art, by St John.

GOD: Noah, take now thy family
And into the ship with thee,
For none so righteous to me
Is now on earth living.

Of clean beasts with thee thou must take
Seven and seven, for my sake,
He and she, mates to make,
These are what you must bring.

Of beasts unclean two and two,
Male and female, in counting be true.
Of clean fowls seven bring through
Then, he and she together.

Of fowls unclean two and no more
As of the beasts I said just before.
These shall be saved from dangers sore
When I send the bad weather.

Of all the meats that must be eaten
Now into the hold see they be gotten;
For that must not at all be forgotten.
And do this full soon.

To sustain man and beast withal
Until the waters shall cease and fall.
This world is sinful in all
As I see each noon.

Seven days are yet coming
For you to gather and bring
Those after my liking
When mankind I annoy.

Forty days and forty nights
Rain shall fall for their unrights
And those I have made through my mights
Now think I to destroy.

NOAH: Lord, at your bidding I am true
Since grace is only in you,
As you ask I will do.
For gracious I you find.

One hundred winters and twenty
This ship making, tarried have I
Lest through amendment any mercy
Should fall to mankind.

Have done, you men and women all
Hurry lest the waters fall,
See each beast fast into his stall
And safe in our ship brought.

Of clean beasts seven shall be;
Of unclean two, as God bade me;
The flood is nigh, as ye may well see,
Therefore tarry you naught.

   *(The family and animals enter the ark)*

SEM: Sir, here are lions, leopards in,
 Horses, mares, ox and swine,
 Goats, calves, sheep and kine
 Here sitting thou mayst see.

HAM: Camels, asses, men may find,
 Buck, doe, hart and hind,
 And beasts of all other kind
 Are here, it seems to me.

JAPHET: Look here cats and dogs all go,
 Otter, fox, fulmart also,
 Hares hopping gaily on toe
 Have plenty here to eat.

MOTHER NOAH: And here are bears, and wolves a set,
 Apes, owls and marmoset,
 Weasels, squirrels and ferret,
 Here they have eaten their meat.

SEM'S WIFE: Yet more beasts are in this house.
   Here are cats who all carouse
   Here are rats and there a mouse.
   Lo! they stay close together.


HAM'S WIFE: And here are greater and lesser fowls,
   Herons, cranes, bitterns, owls,
   Swans, peacocks, and in those bowls
   Food for this weather.


JAPHET'S WIFE: Here are cocks, kites, crows,
   Rooks, ravens, and many rows
   Of ducks, curlews, whoever knows
   Each one in his kind?


   And here come doves, ducks, drakes,
   Redshanks running up from the lakes;
   For every fowl that birdsong makes
   In this ship we can find.


NOAH: Wife, come! why standest thou there?
   Thou art always froward, that I dare swear.
   Now come, a God's name, time it were
   For fear lest we drown.


MOTHER NOAH: Yea, Sir, set up your sail
   And row forth, so hearty and hale,
   For, without any fail,
   I will not out of our town.


   For I have my gossips everyone.
   One foot further I will not be gone
   For they shall not drown, by St. John,
   If I may save their life.

They love me full well, by Christ,
Though thou wilt not let them in this chest,
So you row forth, Noah, when you list
And get thee a new wife.

NOAH: Sem, son, thy mother is raw, lo,
In truth such a trouble I do not know.

SEM: Father, I will fetch her in, I trow,
Without any fail.

Mother, my father after thee does send
To bid thee upon into the ship to wend.
Look up and see the wind.
We are ready to sail.

MOTHER NOAH: Son, go back to him and say
I will not step inside today.

NOAH: Come in, wife! Oh, your devilish way!
Or else stay there without.

HAM: Shall we fetch her in?

NOAH: Yes, sons, with Christ's blessing and mine:
For here comes of the rain a first sign,
And of this flood I am in no doubt.

JAPHET: Mother, we pray you altogether
Since we are here your own childer,
Come into the ship for fear of the weather
For his love that you has bought.

MOTHER NOAH: That will I not for all your call
Unless I have my gossips all.

SEM: In faith, mother, yet you shall,
　Whether you will or not. *(Forces her in)*


NOAH: Welcome at last into our boat.


MOTHER NOAH: Now take that to thy note.

*(Boxes his ears)*

NOAH: Ha! marry, this is too hot,
　It is good to be still!

　Ah! children, me thinks the boat doth give;
　Tarrying here me much doth grieve
　While over the land the waters do spread
　God does as he will!

　Ah! great God that art so good.
　He that does not thy will is but a clod.
　Now all the world is in a flood
　As I see well in sight.

　This window I will shut anon
　And into my chamber now be gone
　Till this water, Most Great One,
　Slacks off through thy might.

　　　　*(Closes window. Sings from Psalm 79)*

　Now forty days are fully gone
　Send I a raven will anon:
　If anywhere, earth, tree or stone
　Is dry in any place. *(Opens window)*

　And if this bird come not again,
　It is a sign, I maintain.
　That it is dry on hill or plain
　And God has sent his grace. *(Raven sent out)*

Ah, Lord, wherever this raven be
That place is dry, well we see;
But now a dove, by my loyalty
After her will I send.                 (*Dove despatched*)

Ah, Lord, blessed be thou aye,
That hast given us comfort here today!
For now I truly can say
This flood begins to cease.

My sweet dove has brought apace
A branch of olive from some place
Which proves that God has shown us grace
And is a sign of peace.

Ah, Lord, honoured must thou be,
All earth dries now I can see,
But till thou commandest to me
Hence I will not hie.

All the water is away
Therefore as soon as I may
Sacrifice I shall this day
To thee devoutly.

GOD: Noah, take thy wife anon,
And thy children every one;
Out of the ship thou shalt be gone
And all with thee.

Beasts and all that can fly
Out from here may hie
To earth to grow and multiply
I will that it be so.

NOAH: Lord, I thank thee for thy might.
   Thy bidding shall be done in the height.
   For thy mercies, Lord, as is right,
   I will do thee honour.

   For to offer thee sacrifice
   Come all in this manner wise,
   For of the beasts that are his
   I offer back this store.        (*Offerings made on altar*)

GOD: Noah, to me thou art full able
   And thy sacrifice acceptable;
   For I know thee to be true and stable,
   Of thee must I be mindful.

   Worry earth I will no more
   Though man's sin grieves me still sore
   And the youthful as of yore
   Are always found sinful.

   You shall now grow and multiply
   The earth again shall edify
   And beast and fowl that fly
   Shall live in fear of you.

   And fish swimming in the sea
   Shall feed you, believe you me,
   To eat all these you are quite free
   They are clean as you may know.

   My Bow between you and me
   In the firmament shall be
   As a true token for all to see
   That this vengeance shall cease.

That man and woman shall never more
Be devastated by water as before.
For sin that grieveth me sore
Remember the vengeance was.

Where clouds in the skies have been
That new bow shall be seen
In token that my wrath and spleen
Never again shall wreakèd be.

The string is turned towards you
And towards me is bent the bow
That such weather shall never show,
And this promise I thee.

My blessing now I give thee here
To thee, Noah, my servant dear.
For vengeance shall no more appear.
And now fare well, my darling dear.

#### END OF THIRD PLAY

### 4.  ABRAHAM AND ISAAC

GOD: Now Noah away from earth is sent,
    Now hearken all to my new intent.
    Tis Abraham through my great grace
    That is coming to this place.

    Abraham, my servant Abraham!

ABRAHAM: Lo, Lord already here I am.

GOD: Take Isaac, thy son by name
   That thou lovest best of all
   And in sacrifice offer him to me
   Upon that hill beside thee.
   Abraham, I will that it be so
   For aught that may befall.

ABRAHAM: My lord, to thee is my intent
   Always to be obedient;
   That son that thou hast sent
   Offer I will to thee.

   To fulfil thy commandment
   With hearty will was I lent.
   High God, Lord omnipotent,
   Thy bidding done shall be.

   My family and children each one
   Remain at home, every one
   Save Isaac shall with me be gone
   To a hill here beside.

   Make thee ready, my Darling
   For we must do a little thing.
   This wood upon thy back thou bring,
   We must not long abide.

   A sword and fire I will take,
   For sacrifice I must make:
   God's bidding I will not forsake
   But ever obedient be

ISAAC: Father I am all ready
   To do your bidding meekly.
   To bear the wood full set am I
   As you command me.

ABRAHAM: O Isaac, Isaac, my darling dear
My blessing now I give thee here.
Take up this faggot with good cheer
And on thy back it bring.
Here the fire with me I take.

ISAAC: Your bidding I will not forsake,
Father, I will never be slack
To fulfil your bidding.

(ISAAC *takes the wood on his shoulder*)

ABRAHAM: Now, Isaac, dear son, we go our way
To yonder mountain as fast as we may.

ISAAC: My dear father, I will assay
To follow your way.

ABRAHAM: O, my heart will break in three!
To hear thy words I have pity.
As thou wilt, Lord, so must it be
For thee I will obey.

Lay down thy faggot, my own dear son.

ISAAC: All ready, father, look it is here.
But why make you such heavy cheer?
Does anything make you dread?

Father now, if it be your will,
Where is the beast that we shall kill?

ABRAHAM: There is none, son, upon this hill
That I can see to strike dead.

ISAAC: Father, I am full sore afraid
To see your sword thus arrayed.
I hope, by all that is made,
You will not slay your child.

ABRAHAM: My child, I bid thee not dread:
Our Lord will send of his Godhead
Some kind of beast here instead,
Be it tame or wild.

ISAAC: Father, tell me ere I go
Whether I shall be harmed here or no.

ABRAHAM: Ah, dear God, this is such woe
As will burst my heart in sunder.

ISAAC: Father, tell me what is amiss,
Why your sword is drawn out like this.
This naked blade frightens me, I wis,
And I am filled with deep wonder.

ABRAHAM: Isaac, son, peace! I pray thee,
Thou breakest my heart quite in three.

ISAAC: I pray you keep nothing from me
But tell me what you think.

ABRAHAM: O Isaac, Isaac, I must thee kill.

ISAAC: Alas, father, is that your will,
Your own child's life here to spill
Upon this hill's brink?

If I have trespassed in any degree
With a stick now beat me;
Put up your sword, oh, hear my plea
For I am but a child.

ABRAHAM: O my son, I am sorry
To do any hurt, my dear, unto thee,
But God's command is laid upon me.
His works are all mild.

ISAAC: Would God my mother were here now with me;
  She would kneel upon her knee
  To pray you, father, if't might be
  To save her son's life.

ABRAHAM: O comely creature, unless I thee kill
  I offend my God and that sore and ill.
  I may not work against his high will
  But ever obedient be.

  O Isaac, son, to thee I say,
  God has commanded me this day
  Sacrifice—he will not take nay—
  To make of this body.

ISAAC: Is it God's will I should be slain?

ABRAHAM: Yea, son, we must not complain.
  True to his bidding I must ever remain,
  Bound to his pleasing.

  But that I do this doleful deed
  My Lord will not come to me in my need.

ISAAC: Marry, father, God forbid!
  Make now an offering.

  Father, at home your sons you shall find
  That you must love in human kind.
  When I am gone soon out of your mind,
  Your sorrow may soon cease.

  But you must do God's bidding.
  Tell my mother nothing.

ABRAHAM: For sorrow I must my hands wring,
  Thy mother this will not please.

O Isaac, blessed must thou be.
Almost my wits I have lost for thee;
The blood of thy body so free
I am loth now to shed.


ISAAC: Father, since you needs must do so,
  Let it pass quickly as it go;
  Kneeling here before you low
  Your blessing on me spread.                    (*Kneels*)


ABRAHAM: My blessing, dear son, give I thee
  And thy mother's with heart so free.
  The blessing of the Trinity,
  My dear son, light on thee.


ISAAC: I pray you, father, cover my eyen
  That I see not your sword so keen;
  That stroke must not be seen.
  Say no more now to me.


For truly, father, this talking
Does make such long tarrying.
I pray, come now make an ending.
Gone let me be.


ABRAHAM: My dear son, let be thy moans;
  My child, thou grieved me but once.
  Blessed be thou, body and bones,
  Of this deed I am sorry.                       (*Binds him*)


Lord, I would fain work thy will.
This young innocent that lies so still
I am indeed full loth him to kill
In any manner of way.

ISAAC: A mercy, father, why tarry you so?
   Smite off my head and let me go!
   I bid you rid me of all my woe,
   That is all I pray.

   My dear father, I you pray,
   Let me take my clothes away.
   Fear shedding blood on them today
   At my last ending.          (ANGEL *appears*)

ANGEL: Abraham, my servant dear.

ABRAHAM: Lo, lord, I am already here.

ANGEL: Lay not thy sword in no manner
   On Isaac, thy dear darling.

   Nay! do him no injury.
   For thou dreadest God, well I see
   That on thy son thou hast no mercy
   To do his bidding.

   And since his bidding thou doest this day
   And sparest nothing in the heat of this fray,
   To do thy son to death in this way,
   Isaac to thee full dear,

   Therefore God has sent this way
   A lamb that is both good and gay
   Into this place, as see thou may.
   Lo, it is right here!

ABRAHAM: Ah, Lord of heaven and King of bliss,
   Thy bidding I shall do in this.
   Sacrifice here to me sent is
   And all, Lord, through thy grace.

A horned wether here I see
Among the briars tied is he.
Offered to thee it shall be
Anon right in this place.

GOD: Abraham, by my self I swear
Thou hast been so obedient e'er
And spared not thy son so dear
To fulfil my bidding.

Thou shalt be blessed, thou art worthy
Thy seed I shall multiply,
As the stars and sand, so say I,
Of thy body coming.

To enemies shalt thou be severe
And thy seed shall be held in fear
For thou hast been brave here
To do as I thee bade.

And all nations, believe thou Me,
Blessed ever more shall be
Through fruit that shall come of thee
And all the good be made glad.

END OF FOURTH PLAY

# PART II

## 5. THE NATIVITY

GABRIEL: Hail Mary, maiden free,
Full of grace, The Lord is with thee,
Among all women blessed be thou
And blessed the fruit of thy body.

MARY: Ah! Lord that rules land and sea
Who wondrously now surprises me,
A simple maiden of my degree
To be greeted so graciously.

GABRIEL: Mary, fear thou not this day
For thou hast found with high Godhead
A grace far above all other maid
Now, Mary, make thee no moan.

Thou shalt conceive and bear, I tell thee,
A child and his name Jesu shall be.
No one so great shall be as He
And called God's own son.

Our Lord God, believe thou me,
Shall give him his father David's see
To reign forever in Jacob's house he
With full might evermore.

And he that shall be born of thee
Endless life in him shall be,
That such renown and royalty
Was never seen here before.

MARY: How may this be? angel so bright.
For sinfully I never knew any wight.

GABRIEL: The Holy Ghost upon thee shall light
From God in majesty.

Thou art now so seemly in sight
And shalt be full holy in might
When thou shalt bear God's son aright
That Jesu shall be.

Elizabeth that barren was
As thou mayst see conceived has
In age, a son through God's grace,
Forerunner to be of bliss.

MARY: Now since God will have it so be
And such grace has sent to me
Blessed forever shall he be
To please him I cannot miss.                    (*Exit*)

JOSEPH: Alas, alas, and woe is me!
Who hath made her with child?

Well I feared an old man and a may
Could find accord in no way,
These many years I have had no play
Or worked any works so wild.

Three months she hath been from me
And now she has gotten, as I see,
A great belly for her fee
Since she went away.

And mine it is not, I make so bold
For I am both old and cold;
This thirty winter though I would
I have played no such play.

Therefore will I sleep a while.
Now my wife will me beguile
I will go from her; to defile
Myself I am loth, I may say.

This case makes me so heavy
That sleep now craves this eye
Lord, thou on her have mercy
For her misdeed today.                    (*He falls asleep*)

ANGEL: Joseph, leave that feeble thought,
Take Mary, thy wife, and fear thee naught
For wickedly she has not wrought.
This is God's will.

That child that she shall bear, I wis,
Of the Holy Ghost begotten is
To save mankind that did amiss
A prophecy to fulfil.

JOSEPH: Ah, now I know, Lord, it is so.
No man will dare to be her foe.
While I on earth may go
With her I shall be.

Now Christ is come into our fold
As ancient prophets all foretold.
To thy light, Lord, I hold,
And ever worship Thee.

ANGEL: Joseph, I warn thee as I may
  To Bethlem thou must take thy way
  Lest in danger thou fallest today
  If thou beest long.

JOSEPH: Now since it must no other be,
  Mary, dear wife, now hurry we.
  An ox will I take off with me
  Which there can be sold.

  The money from him, it seems to me
  Shall help us in this city
  And pay for both the tribute fee
  In silver and gold.

              (*They leave and come to stable*)

MARY: Ah, Lord, what may all this be?
  Some men I see glad and merry
  While some sigh and are sorry.
  Wheresoever it be.

  Since God's son man's soul to buy
  Is come through his great mercy
  Methinks man should take kindly
  This sight gladly to see.

ANGEL: Mary, God's mother dear,
  This token I hope to show clear.
  The common people thou seest here
  Are glad as they well may.

  For they shall see of Abraham's seed
  Christ come to help in their hour of need.
  Therefore they joy and are glad
  To have seen this day.

The mourning men—bear this in mind—
Are Jews that shall be left behind.
No more for them is the Law designed.
Now Christ is coming.

They shall have more grace to know
That God's care for man has stooped so low;
For their shame on them that soon shall show.
Now they sit mourning.

JOSEPH: Mary, sister, the truth now to say
   No shelter I see for us here today,
   For lords of stout array
   Occupy this city.

Therefore we must, in good fay,
Lie in this stable till it be day.
To make men meek, believe it I may
Come here to be born will He.

MARY: Help me down, my husband dear,
   For I fear my time is near;
   Christ in this poor stable here
   Now born will be.

JOSEPH: Come to me, my sweet dear,
   Heaven's treasure is here.
   Welcome in full meek manner.
   Him I hope now to see.

Mary, my love, I will assay
To get two midwives if but I may
For though in thee be God verray
Come to our kind.

I shall discover in this city
Two I can fetch here to thee.
Their help you will need at once I see
As soon as I can find.

*(JOSEPH walks to Midwives)*

Women, God save you, praise be,
Is it your will to come with me?
My wife is now come to this city
With child.  Her time is near.

Help her now, for charity,
And stay with her till day be.
For your pains, now promise I thee,
I will pay you right here.

TEBELL: All ready, good man, let us away,
We will do whatever we may
For two such fine midwives, I say,
Are not in this city.

SALOME: Come, good man, lead you the way,
With God's help, before break of day,
If we acted well, thy wife shall say
And that thou shalt see.                    *(Return to stable)*

JOSEPH: Lo! Mary, dear heart, I have here
Two midwives to bring thee some cheer
And stay with thee, my darling dear,
Till it be day.                    *(Pause: the star appears)*

MARY: Ah, Joseph, tidings are right.
I have a son, the sweetest wight.
I give thanks, Lord, to thy great might.
God's son here I lay.

JOSEPH: Lord, welcome, sweet Jesu!
  Thy name thou hast before I thee knew
  For now I know the Angel spoke true
  Upon that glad day.

MARY: Lord, blessed must thou be
  That are simple born as I see;
  To rob the devil of mastery
  The angel did say.

  Fine clothes are not for thee,
  Therefore thy sweet body free
  In this manger shalt lie near me
  And lapped round with hay.

TEBELL: Ah, dear Lord, Heaven-King,
  This is indeed a marvellous thing
  Without groan or travailing
  A fair son is born.

SALOME: Ah, sweet Child I ask mercy
  For thy mother's love, Mary,
  For all in my life I did wickedly
  Sweet Child, forgive it me.

  Ah, blessed be God, all happy am I
  Now I know well and steadfastly
  That God is come mankind to buy
  And thou, Lord, thou art he.

**END OF FIFTH PLAY**

## 6.  THE ADORATION OF THE SHEPHERDS

1ST SHEPHERD: Oh! with walking weary I have me wrought
  Over the hills my sheep have I sought.
  Sickening beasts are in my thought
  How to save them and heal.

  From the scabs they have caught
  Or the rot, have I fought
  And the cough as I ought.
  For each one do I feel.

  Lo! here be my herbs, safe and sound
  Wisely wrought for every wound,
  And could a sound man bring to ground
  Within a little while!

  Here henbane and horehound,
  Ribbie, radish and egremont,
  These are my herbs, safe and sound
  Mixed all in a row.

  Here be more herbs, I tell it you.
  I will add these to the others too,
  Finter, fanter and fetterfoe,
  Also a penny wort.

  This is all that I can do
  If it be wether or if it be ewe;
  All their sore ills this will undo
  And clean up all hurt.

  But no fellowship here have I
  Save myself all alone upon high.
  And now for a meal I do die,
  But first for a drink if I may.                    (*Drinks*)

Ho! Hullo, there, ho, ho!
Drive all the sheep down low.
They may not hear unless I do blow;
Now out my horn shall bay.                    (*Blows horn*)

2ND SHEPHERD: Hullo, now be well met!
One thing only we need is
That Tod here should be set
Then we might sit and feed us.

1ST SHPEHERD: Call him, " Tod, Tibb's son "
Ay, then he will come,
For he will always run
At his mother's name.

2ND SHPEHERD: Now, Tod! Tibb's son!

3RD SHEPHERD: Sir, see, here I come
Though I have not all done
What I have begun.

To store salve for our sheep
Into an old wide-necked can.
Now with gravel piled deep
I must scour an old pan!

Now, good friends, it is not unknown
To husbands that live hereabout
That our wives may all moan
And often reach us with a clout.

Hankin, hold up thy hand and help me
To stand on that height there by thee.

1ST SHEPHERD: Gladly, Tod, if you will come here by me
For I am sure I would never deny thee.

2ND SHEPHERD: Now since God has gathered us together
  With good heart I thank Him for His grace.
  Welcome are you as is fair weather:
  Tod, shall we all take some solace?

3RD SHEPHERD: Ay, here is bread this day was made,
  Onions, garlic and leeks,
  Butter and eggs this day were laid
  And green cheese to grease your cheeks.

  And here ale of Halton I have
  And what meat I had for my hire;
  A pudding may no man deprave
  And an oat-cake from Lancashire.

  Look, here's a sheep's head soused in ale
  And a loin to lay on the green,
  And sour milk my wife had on sale
  A noble supper as may be seen.

1ST SHEPHERD: And as it is seen, ye shall see
  What things I have here in my sack:
  A pig's foot I have here, pardee!
  A dish of cold tripe in my pack.

  A sausage, fellows, now have I,
  A liver too I do not lack;
  Chitterlings boiled this must be.
  Such burden I bear on my back.

1ST SHEPHERD: Let us all eat here right gladly:     (*They eat*)
  Away with all our grousing.
  Come eat with us, God from Heaven on high,
  Take no heed that here be no housing.

2ND SHEPHERD: Housing enough have we here
  While we have heaven over our heads;
  Now to wet our mouths time it were.
  This flagon I broach, no more said.          (*Star appears*)


1ST SHEPHERD: What is all this light here
  That shines so bright here
  On my black beard?
  For to see this sight here
  A man may take fright here
  For I am afraid.


2ND SHEPHERD: Afraid for a fray now,
  That we all may now;
  Yet is it night
  Though seems it day now,
  Never, truly to say now
  Saw I such a sight.


3RD SHEPHERD: Such a sight seeming
  And a light gleaming,
  I am afraid to look.
  All this bright beaming
  From a star streaming.
  I am sore struck.


ANGEL: Gloria in excelsis Deo
  Et in terra pax
  Hominibus bonae voluntatis.


  Shepherds, of this sight
  Be ye not afright
  For this is God's might,
  Take this in mind!

To Bethlehem go now right
There you shall see in sight
That Christ is born tonight
To redeem all mankind.          (*They move to Bethlehem*)


1ST SHEPHERD: To Bethlehem take the way.
    Over the hills let us wend
    That prince of peace to pray
    Heaven to have at our end.


3RD SHEPHERD: Sim! Sim! Securely
    Here I see Mary
    And Jesu Christ fast by,
    Lapped in the hay.


2ND SHEPHERD: Kneel we down all three
    And pray we him for mercy;
    And welcome him worthily
    That drives woe away.


1ST SHEPHERD: Whatever does this old man that here is,
    See how his head is bent before,
    His beard shows like a brush of briars
    And a pound of hair round his mouth and more.


2ND SHEPHERD: More is the marvel to me now
    To take a nap here greatly he needs.
    Full sleepy and worn is that brow
    Tired out with these wondrous deeds.


3RD SHEPHERD: Lo! though his beard be rough
    How well to her look he heeds;
    Worthy wight, truth would we know
    Why here the bright star shepherd leads.

MARY: Shepherds, truly I see
   That my son you hither sent,
   Through God's might and majesty
   That by me to the world is lent.
   This man married was to me
   For no sin or such assent,
   But to keep my virginity,
   And truly in no other intent.

JOSEPH: Good men, Moses take in mind,
   As he was made through God's great might,
   Ordained laws as to bind,
   Which we should keep of right,
   Man and woman for to bind
   Lawfully them both to light,
   To fructify, as men may find;
   That time was wedded every wight.

   Therefore wedded to her I was,
   As law would, her to be near,
   To end noise, slander and trespass,
   And through that deed the devil to dare,
   As told me Gabriel, full of grace;
   That she was lackless of sin;
   And when I heard this case
   From her I could never win.

   Therefore go and preach forth this thing,
   All together, with kith and kin,
   That you have seen your heavenly King
   Come, all mankind to win.

1ST SHEPHERD: Come we near anon,
   With such as we have brought,
   Ring, brush or precious stone;
   Let's see whether we have aught.

2ND SHEPHERD: Let us do him homage.

1ST SHEPHERD: Lo! I bring thee a bell;
   I pray thee, save me from hell
   That I may with thee dwell
   And fare well for aye.

2ND SHEPHERD: I bring thee a flask and a spoon
   To eat thy pottage withal at noon
   As I myself so oft have done.
   With heart, I pray thee, take it.

3RD SHEPHERD: The gift I bring thee is but small
   Though I come up last of all.
   I bring but a cap to thy stall,
   But Lord, think still on me.

1ST SHEPHERD: Now farewell, mother and may,
   For of sin naught thou knowest,
   Thou hast brought forth this day
   God's son which in might is the most.

2ND SHEPHERD: Brethren, let us all three,
   Singing, walk homewards.
   Unkind will I never be
   But preach what I can and cry
   As Gabriel taught by his grace to me,
   Singing always hence will I.

3RD SHEPHERD: Over the sea, and I may have grace,
   I will pass and about go now
   To preach this in every place;
   And sheep will I keep no more now.

1ST SHEPHERD: And I an hermit
   Praise to God to pay,
   To walk by stye and street,
   In wilderness to walk for aye;

And I shall no man meet
But for my living I will him pray,
Barefooted on my feet;
And thus will I live ever and aye.

3RD SHEPHERD: To that bliss bring us,
Great God, if it thy will be
Amend all things that are amiss.
Good men, now farewell to ye.

1ST SHEPHERD: Well to fare, too, dear friend,
God of his might grant to you;
For here now we make an end.
Farewell for we from you must go too.

**END OF SIXTH PLAY**

7.   ADORATION OF THE MAGI

1ST KING: Mighty God in majesty
That ruled the people of Judee,
When thou on man wilt have mercy
As I can foresee,

Send some token, Lord, to me
That some star we may see
That Balaam said should rise and be
In his prophecy,

For well I know of this,
That his prophecy truth is:
A star should rise betokening bliss
When God's son is born.

Therefore these Lords and I all here
On this mount make our prayer
Devoutly once in the year
For thus we have sworn.


2ND KING: Yea, we that be of Balaam's blood,
That prophesied once of that sweet food
When Balak, that man of no good,
A curse would have made


To God's people of Israel.
But power him did fail
To prophesy men's heal
What God to Balaam had said


Therefore we kings of his kind
I advise, we keep his words in mind.
Thanks to him if we find
That God's son shall be.


Now go to pray, one and all,
To that Mount Victorial.
Peradventure grace may fall
And that star we may see.


3RD KING: Sir, you advise us all right;
Upon that hill now this night
We will beseech God Almight
On us to have mind,


And of that star to gain sight
So to worship that wight
Whose birth Balaam saw bright
To buy back all mankind.                    (*Pray on mountain*)

1ST KING: Lord God, Leader of Israel,
    That would die man to heal,
    Come thou to us not to conceal
    But be our counsellor.

2ND KING: Who all this world shalt make well
    And shall be called Emmanuel
    Grant us, Lord, with thee to dwell
    And hear now our prayer.        *(Star appears)*

ANGEL: Ah! rise up ye kings three
    And come after me
    Into the land of Judee
    As fast as you may hie!

    The child you seek you shall see
    Born of a maiden free
    That King of heaven and earth shall be
    All man back to buy.        *(Mount and depart)*

1ST KING: Ah, where is the path of the star?
    That light is away from us far:
    In the dark we may mar
    And lose quite our way.

3RD KING: It were best we enquire
    Now we lack the star's fire.
    Say, Belamy, that rides there,
    Tell us some tiding.

MESSENGER: Tell me, sir, what your wills are.

1ST KING: Canst thou say what place or where
    A child is born that crown to bear
    And of the Jews be the King?

2ND KING: We saw a star shine verray
  In the East in noble array
  And we are come all this way
  Our joy here to win.

MESSENGER: Hold you peace, sirs, I you pray,
  For if King Herod heard you so say
  He would go mad, by my fay,
  And fly out of his skin.

3RD KING: And since a King is so near
  We go to him to inquire.

MESSENGER: You may well see he lives here,
  In this palace does he dwell.

  But should he know, in this hour
  One is born of more power
  He would rage loud in his tower
  If this one should tell.

        *(To* HEROD)

  O noble King and worthy conqueror
  Crowned in gold, sitting on high,
  Mahound thee save long in honour:
  Thy leave I ask to come nigh.

  Tidings now, my Lord, I shall tell
  That these three kings do tell unto me;
  Though whence they be I know not well.
  Yonder they stand as you may see.

1ST KING: Sir, we saw the star appear
  In the East over here
  In marvellous manner
  Together, as we can say.

2ND KING: We saw never none so clear
    And from its ray we came here
    But when we came this land near
    Then vanished it away.

3RD KING: By prophecies well all know we
    That a child born should be
    To rule the people of Judee
    As we have believed many a year.

HEROD: I am king of kings, none so keen;
    I the sovereign sir as may be seen,
    I tyrant, wherever I have been,
    Take castle, tower and town.

    I wield all this world in my power,
    I beat all who disobedient are,
    I drive the devils and scatter afar
    Then into Hell I send down.

    For I am king of all mankind;
    I bid, I beat, I loose, I bind,
    I master the moon, take this in mind
    That I am most in might.

    I am the greatest above degree
    That is or was or ever shall be.
    The sun it dare not shine upon me
    If I bid him go down.

    Nor shall the rain to fall be free
    Nor no lord have that liberty
    That dare abide if I bid flee
    For I shall crack his crown.

                         (*Flourishing spear, shield, etc.*)

But since you spoke of prophecy
I will call in here to see
Whether you tell the truth or a lie
For that my clerk will tell me.

(*To* DOCTOR)

These kings are come a long way
To seek a child, I heard them say,
That should be born in this country
My kingdom to destroy.

Turn every leaf I here thee pray
And what thou findest, in good fay,
Tell me here, for I dare lay
That all these lords lie.

DOCTOR: Nay my lord, be you so good,
   I think no prophet to write ever could
Words on this matter that should
Your great right deny.

But since your Grace at this time would
That I to state the prophecy should,
Of Christ's coming as they have told
The truth to certify.

The holy scripture maketh declaration
By patriarchs and prophets of Christ's nativity,
When Jacob prophesied by plain demonstration
That the realm of Juda and also regality
From that generation should never taken be,
Till he should come who most mighty is,
Sent from the Father, the King of Heaven's bliss.

And now fulfilled is Jacob's prophecy
For King Herod that is now reigning
Is no Jew born, nor of that progeny,

But a stranger, by the Romans made King
By succession to claim the sceptre and royalty:
Wherefore Christ is born, King-Messiah is He!

HEROD: That is false, by Mahound's great might!
That old villain Jacob, a dotard in age,
Shall withhold by no prophecy the title and right
Of Roman's high conquest which to me in heritage
And fallen forever, as a prince of high parentage.
If any other King-Messiah intends it to win
His head from his body with this sharp sword I'll pin.

Ah! never such slaughter was seen or heard before
Since Athaliah here reigned, that fell, furious Queen,
Who killed all male children that royal blood bore,
When her son was dead, as when I wreak my spleen
I shall hew that young devil with bright brand so keen
Into pieces small.  I shall search till I find
That presumptuous page and shall kill as I have designed.

What a devil! is this to say
I should be disproved and put away
Since my right is clear as day.
All for a boy's boast!
This realm is mine and shall be aye,
Manfully to maintain while I may,
Though he bring with him today
The devil and all his host.

But go ye forth, ye Kings three,
And enquire if so it be,
And anyway come back here to me
For you I hope to feed.
And if he be of such degree
Him will I honour as also do ye,
As befits his high dignity
In thought, word and deed.

1ST KING: We leave, sir.  Have good day
  Till we come again this way.


2ND KING: Sir, as soon as ever we may,
  As we have seen, so shall we say.


3RD KING: And of his riches and his array
  We shall make all quite plain,


HEROD: Farewell, Lords, in good fay!
  And come soon again.                    (*Exeunt*)
  By my soul, come they again,
  Those three traitors shall all be slain
  And also that swaddling swain
  I shall swipe off his head.
  God's grace shall never them gain
  Nor prophecy save them from pain!
  I will rock that ribald that I may reign
  And he shall rue all I have said.
  Fill fast and let the cups fly
  And go we hither hastily,
  For I must ordain curiously
  Against these Kings' coming.
  This boast does me so great annoy
  That I wax dull and pure dry;
  Have done, and fill the wine up high,
  I die but I have drink!


### END OF SEVENTH PLAY

## 8.  THE MAGI'S OBLATION

*THE KINGS are led by the star towards the stable*

1ST KING: The star yonder over the stable is;
    I pray we be not gone amiss,
    For it has always moved ere this
    And now that way it is bent.

2ND KING: I deem he dwells here, I wis,
    And this simple house is his.
    Offer we now that King of bliss
    At once our present.

3RD KING: What present will best for him fall,
    Cast we here betwixt us all;
    For though he lie in an ox-stall
    His might is never the less.

1ST KING: By gold, that we bring to this town,
    That richest metal of renown,
    Skilfully understand we now
    Most precious Godhead.
    And incense may well be shown
    A root of great devotion,
    By Myrrh, that waives corruption,
    Clean flesh, both quick and dead.

    Now we have proved it here,
    These gifts to him be most dear,
    Go we forth in good manner
    And make we our present.

2ND KING: The Star it shines fair and clear
    Overhead as we draw near.
    His dwelling now I know is here,
    And herein he is lent.

3RD KING: A fair maiden, sirs, yonder I see,
    An old man sitting at her knee,
    A child also, as thinks me,
    Three persons are therein.

1ST KING: I say certain: this is he
    That we have sought from our country;
    Therefore now with all honesty
    Honour will I that bairn.
    Hail be thou, Lord Christ and Messy
    That from God art come kindly
    Mankind of woe back to buy
    And into bliss to bring.

2ND KING: Hail be thou, Christ Emmanuel,
    That art come for man's heal
    And for to win against that wail
    That Adam put away.

3RD KING: Hail, Conqueror of all mankind!
    To do mercy thou hast mind
    The Devil's bands to unbind
    And relieve all thine.

*(They kneel and present their gifts)*

MARY: You royal kings in rich array,
    The high Father of Heaven I pray
    To reward your good deed today,
    For his powerful might,
    And give you, now and always,
    To yearn for life that lasteth aye,
    And never to fall out of the fay
    That in you glows so bright.

    Believe, Lords, as you come near
    That to my son you shall be dear
    That Him today hath honoured here
    And me also for his sake.

When the time is come entire
To prove his strength and his power
To him you shall be known most dear,
That dare I undertake.

JOSEPH: You Kings all, chiefs of mankind,
Full faithfully you shall it find:
These gifts God will have in mind
And requite you in your need.
Believe you well, bear this in mind,
He is not gotten like all mankind;
They that think it are full blind
For I know it in deed.


You must know forsooth, I wis,
Clean maiden that she is
And with man did never amiss,
And thereof be you bold.
But of the Holy Ghost this is,
For to bring mankind to bliss,
And this child is verily his
So Gabriel me told.


ANGEL: I warn you, comely Kings three,
My Lord would not that you spilled be,
Therefore he sends you word by me
To turn another way.
Herod's fellowship you shall flee,
For you harm ordained has he.
Therefore go not through his country
Not the path you came today.

1ST KING: Ah, high Lord, that we honour here,
To warn us in this manner!
Else had we gone in no fear
To him that would our blood spill.

2ND KING: Yea, Lord, King without peer
    We will do all in our power.
    Go we hence all in fear
    And his bidding fulfil.


3RD KING: Farewell, Sir Kings, friends so dear,
    I thank you both of your good cheer,
    But my mind is not yet clear
    Lest Herod some trap shall lay.
    He that shaped both sea and sand
    Send us safe into our Land.
    Kings two, give me your hand,
    Farewell, and have good day!                    (*Exuent*)


### END OF EIGHTH PLAY


## 9.   THE SLAYING OF THE INNOCENTS

HEROD: Lo, those false traitors, dark and light,
    Who should have come again tonight,
    By another way have taken their flight;
    This way they durst not take.
    Therefore that boy, by God almight,
    Shall be slain soon in your sight,
    And, though it be against the right,
    A thousand for his sake.


    Alas, what purpose had that page,
    That is so young and tender of age,
    That would bereave my heritage,
    That am so much of might?

Forsooth that shrew was wondrous sage
Against me any war to wage;
That rocked ribald, for all his rage,
Shall not bereave me of my right.

How, petty brat my messenger,
Come hither and quickly stir,
For thou must go without murmur
Into Judea this day,
After my doughty and comely knights
And bid them hie with all their mights,
And that they will not be scant of fights,
Bring them without delay!

PRECO: Yes, my lord of great renown,
To do your word I hurry down
Lightly to leap through dale and town
And speed till I were there.
Farewell, my lord in majesty,
For on your journey I will hie me.                    (*Exit*)

HEROD: Now mighty Mahound be with thee,
Ever to dwell together.

1ST SOLDIER: Hail, comely King, crowned in gold!
No king or kaiser but must bend;
If any were that with your worship were so bold,
Such strokes for your sakes we shall send.

2ND SOLDIER: If we him may take or get,
The devil with him soon shall be met
And so he shall be quit
Such mastery to pretend.

HEROD: Welcome, our knights, that be so gent,
Now will we tell you our intent,
What is the cause we for you sent
So soon and hastily.

Yesterday to this city
When we were in our royalty
There came to us kings three
And told us their intent.

To seek a child that born should be
That was said by prophecy
That should be King of Judee
And many another land.
We gave them leave to search, and see
And come again to this city,
And if he were of such degree
We would not him withstand.

But if they had come back again
All three traitors should have been slain,
And also that litter swain
And all for his sake.
Out alas, what may this be?
For I know not which is he;

Therefore all knave-children in this country
On them shall fall the wreak.
For we know not that child well,
Though we therefore should go to hell,
All the children of Israel
We deem now shall be slain!

Therefore my knights, good and keen,
Have done! look live! go, vent my spleen!
Go, slay that shrew! let it be seen
That you be men of main!

You must hie out of this town
To Bethlem, as fast you can get down.
All knave-children, by my Crown!
Tonight they must be ta'en.

1ST SOLDIER: Alas, Lord, and king of bliss
  Send you after us for this?
  A villainy it were, I wis,
  For my fellow and me.

2ND SOLDIER: My liege lord of great renown,
  We shall kill within the town
  Whether he be knight or champion
  Stiffer that ever Samson was.

HEROD: You shall walk far and near
  Into Bethlem, spare for no beer
  All knave-children within two year
  And one day old.
  Slay them both one and all,
  So shall you meet in his stall
  That one would my kingdom claim and call
  And my wealth also wield.

1ST SOLDIER: It shall be done, Lord in high;
  Shall none be left, truthfully.
  We shall go search by and by
  In Bethlem all about.
  And wreak your spleen full tenderly
  Leave none unslain truthfully,
  So shall we soon that shrew destroy
  And kill him in the rout.

2ND SOLDIER: And I also, without boast,
  Though the King of Scots and all his host
  Were here, I set not by their boast,
  To drive them down at sight.
  I slew ten thousand upon a day
  Of champions in their best array,
  There was not one escaped away
  From my sharp sword so bright.

I would I might find in my way
Samson in his best array,
To look whether I durst affray
To fight with him right here.

HEROD: Nay, nay, I know well what you swear,
That you are a doughty man of war,
And though Samson were here
Right soon he would be slain.          (*Exeunt* SOLDIERS)

(*The* TWO SOLDIERS *enter the town and meet the women with
their children*)

1ST SOLDIER: Have done, fellows, hie fast!
Oh, that these queans were down cast,
And their children to death at last
And cut all into pieces.

2ND SOLDIER: Yea, sir, we dwell all too long;
Therefore go we them among!
They will soon meet some wrong
Before this day ceases.

1ST WOMAN: Whom callest thou " Quean ", scabbed bitch?
My dame thy daughter was never such,
She burned a kiln beside a ditch,
Yet did I never none.

2ND WOMAN: Are you so hardy, before I beat,
To handle my son that is so sweet,
This distaff and thy head shall meet,
Before we are hither gone.

1ST SOLDIER: Dame, abide, and let me see,
A knave child if it be.
The King has commanded me
All such to arrest.

1ST WOMAN: Arrest, robber, by thee?
    Thou liest on my loyalty.
    I advise you hence to flee
    And let me have my peace.

2ND WOMAN: Say, rotten hunter with thy goad,
    Horrid ape, stuck toad!
    I tell thee here no wrong to bode
    Lest thou might beaten be.

2ND SOLDIER: Dame, thy son, in good fay,
    He must of me learn to play;
    He must hop ere I go away,
    Upon my spear end.

1ST WOMAN: Out, out and well away!
    That ever I saw this day!
    One stroke yet I will assay
    To give before I wend.

2ND WOMAN: Out on thee, thief!
    My love, my Lord, my pet, my life,
    Did never man nor woman grieve
    To suffer such torment.
    But revenged will I be:
    Here have one, two and three,
    Bear the King this from me,
    And that I it send.

1ST SOLDIER: Come hither to me, dame Parnell!
    And show me here thy son, Snell,
    For the King has bid me quell
    All we find this noon.

1ST WOMAN: My son, nay, strong thief,
    For if I have good proof
    Do thou my child any grief
    I shall crack thy crown.

                              (*The* SOLDIER *stabs the child*)

Out, out, and woe is me!
Thief, thou shalt hanged be!
My child is dead, now I see,
My sorrow may not cease.
Thou shalt be hanged on a tree
And all thy fellows with thee;
All the men in this country
Shall not make thy peace.
Have thou this, thou foul harlot!
And thou knight, I'll tie the knot,
And one buffet with this foot
Thou shalt have to boot.

2ND SOLDIER: Dame, show me the child there,
He must hop upon my spear,
And if he is male, thy dear,
I must teach him to play.

2ND WOMAN: If thou do me any harm
Or the child upon my arm,
I shall know how to keep thee warm
No matter what thou shalt say.

(*The* SOLDIER *stabs the second boy*)

Out, out, out, out!
You shall be hanged and all your rout,
Thieves, be you never so stout
Full foully you have done.
This child was given to me
To look to. Thieves, woe to ye!
He was not mine as you shall see,
He was the King's son.
I shall tell and you shall sigh,
His child was slain before mine eye.
Thieves, you shall be hanged high,
When I come to his hall.

But ere I go, have thou one,
And thou another, Sir John,
For to the King I will anon
To complain upon you all.          (*She goes to* HEROD)

Look, Lord, look and see,
The child that thou sentst to me,
Men of thy own, now see
Have slain it, with sword keen.

HEROD: Fie, whore, fie, God make thee repine!
Why didst not thou say that child was mine?
But it is vengeance, as drink I wine,
And that is clearly seen.

2ND WOMAN: Yea, Lord, they see well aright,
Thy son was like to have been a knight,
For in harness gold and bright
He was painted wondrous gay.
Yet was I never so sore afright,
When their spears through him did bite;
Lord, so little was my might,
When they began the fray.

HEROD: He was indeed in silk array,
In gold and garments that were gay.
They might well know by his array
He was a King's son.
What the devil! why this today?
Why were thy wits so far away?
Couldst thou not speak? couldst thou not pray?
And say it was my son?

Alas, what the devil, why must I moan?
Alas, my days be now done.
I know I must die soon,
For damned I must be.

My legs are rotting and my arms;
I have done so many harms,
That now I see fiends in swarms
From hell coming for me.
I have done so much woe,
And never good since I might go,
Therefore I see now coming my foe,
To fetch me to hell.
I bequeath here in this place
My soul to be with Satanas.
I die, I die, alas, alas!
I may no longer dwell.                    (*Dies*)

DEVIL: Ware, ware, for now unaware wakes your woe,
For I am swifter than is the doe.
I am come with this Lord to go
In woe ever to dwell.
From Lucifer, that Lord, hither I am sent,
To fetch this King's soul here present,
And to hell bring him there to be lent
Ever to live in woe.
There fire burns, breaks and brands,
He shall be there, this Lord, among the bands,
His place evermore is in our lands,
His body never forth to go,

No more shall you tapsters, by my loyalty,
That fill your measures falsely,
Shall bear this Lord company;
You shall get no more great pay.

I will bring this into woe,
And come again and fetch off more
As fast as ever I may go.
Farewell and have good day!            (*Exit with the body*)


END OF NINTH PLAY

# PART III

## 10.   THE TEMPTATION

SATAN:  Now by my sovereignty I swear
    And the principality I bear,
    By hell's pain when I am there
    Tricks I will assay.

    There is a smart fellow I would draw near
    That walks round everywhere,
    Whose father I can ne'er
    Find one to say.

    What kind of man now is this
    That into the world come is?
    His mother I know did never amiss
    And that now marvels me.

    His father can I not find, I wis,
    For all my craft and smartness,
    It seems he thought heaven were his
    Such a stout sire is he,

    He is a man from foot to crown
    But gotten without corruption,
    So clean of conversation
    Knew I none here before.

    All men of him marvel in town
    As this man goeth up and down
    Clad like a saint in a gown
    He has been honoured therefore.

Avarice none, nor envy
In him could I ever espy,
He has no gold in treasury
And is tempted by no sight.


Pride has he none, nor gluttony
Nor liking for lechery.
His mouth heard I never to lie
Neither day nor night.


My highness he puts behind
For in him no fault can I find;
If he be god in mankind
My craft then fully fails.


For more than man I know that he is
Else somewhat he did amiss;
Save when he is hungry, I wis,
I know not that which him ails.


And this thing I dare truly say
If he were indeed God verray
Hunger could grieve him in no way;
That were against reason.                    (*Enter* JESUS)


Therefore now I must assay
With talk of bread him to betray
For he has fasted many a day
Though meat were in season.


Thou, man, abide and speak with me
God's son if that truly thou be,
Make of these stones that we see
Bread through thy blessing.

JESUS: Satan, I tell truth to thee,
   Bread man lives not only by,
   But through God's word, verily,
   Of his mouth coming.

   Therefore thy time dost thou waste
   To supplant me out of my place
   By meat, as thou madest Adam to taste
   When from bliss was he brought.

   Deceived he was through thee
   But now must thou fail verily.
   Therefore with meat to tempt me
   Shall serve thee of naught.

   Satan, through thy enticement
   Hunger shall not turn my intent;
   For the will of the Omnipotent
   Is my meat without fail.

   And His word perfect sustenance
   To me always, wherever I chance,
   For thou shalt find no variance
   In me that shall avail.

SATAN: Out, alas, what is this?
   My trick fares all amiss
   For hungry I see that he is
   As man should naturally be.

   But through no craft nor smartness
   I may not turn his will, I wis,
   No need of meat nor worldly bliss
   In him ever has he.

But I will seek some subtlety;
Come forth, thou Jesu, come up with me
Unto the holy city,
I have a mission to say.


Very God if that thou be
Now I shall full soon see,
For I shall ordain honour for thee
Before thou wendest away.

(*He leads* JESUS *to the pinnacle of the Temple*)


Say, thou that sittest there on high,
If thou be God's son, be sly,
Come down and I will say I see
That thou hast true mastery.


Thine own angel shall keep thee
Lest thou shalt hurt foot or knee;
Show thy power, let us see
Thou mayest have honour thereby.


JESUS: Satan, truly, to thee I say
It is written that thou never may
Tempt the Lord thy God, in no way,
What matter soever be moved.   (*Descends from the pinnacle*)


SATAN: Alas, woe is me today.
Twice have I failed of my prey.
I was never routed in this way
Nor so foully reproved.


But yet if it be thy will
Go we to play upon this hill.
One other point thou must fulfil
For aught that may befall.

Look about thee now and see
Of all these realms the royalty,
If thou kneel down to honour me
And be thyself the lord of all.

JESUS: Go forth, Satan, go forth, go!
It is written and shall be so,
God thy Lord thou shalt honour so
And serve Him; let that suffice.

SATAN: Out, alas, now me is woe!
For found I never so mighty a foe,
Out upon thee, obstinate, now I go,
I am overcome thrice.
(SATAN *leaves and a group of Disciples, together with Two Jews and a Woman taken in adultery enter*)

1ST JEW: Master, I advise by God almight
That we lead this wretched wight
That was taken thus tonight
In foul adultery.

2ND JEW: Before Jesus in his sight
For to tempt him I fight
To see what he will judge as the right
Or reply unlawfully.

It is good advice, by my fay,
That we catch him by this way,
For if he do her a grace today
He doth it against the law.

And if he bid punish her sore
He does it against his own lore,
That he hath preached here before:
To mercy man shall draw.

(*Approaching* JESUS)

Master, this woman that is here,
Is a wedded wife, have no fear,
But with another than her wedded dear
She was found all amiss.

And Moses' Law bids us stone
All such women as be unclean.
Therefore from thee we all mean
To hear a judgement of this.

JESUS:  Now, which of you everyone
Is without sin, prepare him anon
And cast at her the first stone,
Speak now or hold your peace.

                                    (*He writes on the ground*)

1ST JEW:  Speak on, we wait what you have to say;
Shall she be stoned, yes or nay?
Shall we show her mercy here today
Her sins to regard shall we cease?

2ND JEW:  Master, why are thou so still?
What writest thou? If it be thy will
Whether shall we spare or spill
This woman found in shame?

What writest thou, master? Let me see.
Out, alas, woe is me.
Here no longer dare I be,
For dread of the world's blame!              (*They flee*)

JESUS:  Woman, where be those men each one
That put this guilt thee upon?
To damn thee is there none
Of those that were before.

WOMAN: Lord, to damn me there is none
   For they all away have gone.

JESUS: Neither do I condemn thee; thou, woman,
   Go forth and sin no more.

WOMAN: Ah, Lord, blessed may thou be,
   That in this plight hast helped me.
   From henceforth sin I will flee
   And serve thee in good fay.

   For godhead full in thee I see
   That knoweth all works that may be;
   I honour thee, kneeling on my knee
   And so I will do aye.          (*Exit*)

JESUS: Brethren I am filius Dei, the light of the world;
   He that follows me walks not in darkness
   But hath the light of life, the scriptures record,
   As patriarchs and prophets all bear me witness,
   Both Abraham and Isaac and Jacob in their testimonies,
   Unto whom I was promised, before the world began,
   To pay their ransom and to become man.

   Go we then, brethren, while the day is light
   To do my father's work; as I am minded
   To heal the sick and restore the blind to sight,
   That the prophecy may be fulfilled.
   For other sheep I have, which to me are committed.
   They be not of this flock, yet I will them regard
   That they may be one flock with one shepherd.
                (*Walks off*; MARTHA *follows him*)

MARTHA: Oh, Lord Jesus, hadst thou before been led
   Lazarus my brother had not now been dead.
   But well I know we shall be advised
   Now thou art with us here.

And this I believe and hope aright:
Whatever thou askest of God almight
He will grant it thee in thy right
And answer thy prayer.

JESUS: Martha, thy brother shall rise, I say.

MARTHA: That believe I, Lord, in good fay,
For he shall rise upon the last day
Then hope I him to see.

JESUS: Martha, I tell thee, without nay
I am the rising and the life verray,
His life I say shall last for aye
And never shall ended be.

Whosoever believes steadfastly
In me, I tell thee verily,
Though he dead and buried be
Shall live and fare well.
Believe woman, for this may be.

MARTHA: Thus have I believed steadfastly
Therefore on me now have mercy,
And on my sister too, Mary,
I will fetch her to thee.

(*Enter* MARY)

Ah, Mary, sister, sweetest and dear
Hie thee quickly and come near.
My sweet lord, Jesu, he is here.
Now speak to him too.

MARY: Ah, well were we, by my word,
Had only my wise gracious lord
Seen my brother lie on his bier
Some aid might have been done.

But now he stinketh, truth for to say,
For now this is the fourth day
Since he was buried in the clay,
That to me was so dear.

JESUS: Where have you laid him? come now show me.

MARY: Lord, come hither and thou mayst see
For buried in this place is he
Four days now agone.
                    (*They move to the tomb*; JEWS *return*)

1ST JEW: See follow, for by my soul,
This freak begins to scream and yowl
And make great sound of dole
Since he loved him before.

2ND JEW: If he were clever methinks he might
From death have saved this Lazar by right
As well as sent a man his sight
That was as he was born.

JESUS: Have done, and lift away the stone.

MARTHA: Ah, Lord, four days now be gone
Since he was buried, blood and bone,
He stinks now, Lord, in good fay.

JESUS: Martha, said I not to thee,
That if thou believest wholly in me
God's grace thou soon shouldest see?
Therefore do as I to thee say.     (*They roll back the stone*)

Father of Heaven, I give thanks to Thee,
That so soon Thou has heard from me
Well I know and truly do see
Thou hearest my intent.

But for the people that stand thereby
Speak I the more openly
That they may believe steadfastly
That from heaven was I sent.

Lazarus come forth, I bid thee.                (LAZARUS *rises*)

LAZARUS: Ah, Lord, blest may thou be,
From death to life hast raised me
Through thy great might,

Lord, when I heard the voice of thee
All hell lost its power over me
So fast from them my soul did flee
The devils were afraid.

JESUS: Loose him now and let him go.

MARTHA: Ah, Lord, honoured be thou so
That hast us saved from much woe
As thou hast often before.

MARY: Well I hoped and fears did I fight
When thou camest that all should be right.
Thee, Lord, I honour and now here so low
I kneel upon my knee.

MARTHA: With thee, Lord, ever will I be
And serve thee always with a heart free
That this day hast so gladded me
And won my heart ever to thee.

JESUS: Have good day, my daughters dear,
Wherever you go, far or near,
My blessing I give you here.
To Jerusalem I take now my way.

END OF TENTH PLAY

JESUS: Brethren, go we to Bethany,
    To Lazarus, Martha and Mary,
    For I love much their company
    Whither now will I wend.
    Simon the Leper has prayed me
    In his house to take charity;
    With them now it likes me,
    A while for to spend.

PETER: Lord, all ready shall we be
    In life and death to go with thee.
    Great joy they may have to see
    Thy coming into their place.

PHILIP: Lazar thou raised through thy ability
    And Simon also—a leper was he—
    Thou cleansed, Lord—that know all we—
    And helped through thy grace.

SIMON: Welcome, Jesu, full of grace!
    For me, that foul and leprous was,
    All whole, Lord, thou healed has
    The world all to show.
    Well it is that I may see thy face
    Here in my house, this poor place.
    Thou comfortest me in many a case
    And that I full well know.

LAZARUS: Welcome, Lord, thou sweet Jesu!
    Blessed be the time that I thee knew!
    From death to life, through thy virtue,
    Thou raised me before.

Four days in earth had I lain
When thou grantedst me life again.
Thee I honour with might and main
Now and evermore.


MARTHA: Welcome, my Lord, are you here.
Welcome my dearest friend dear!
Now may thy friends all draw near
To see thy noble face.
If now this is your will clear,
Sit and I shall serve you here
As I was wont in good manner
Before in another place.

> (JESUS *sits and* MARY MAGDALENE *approaches with an alabaster box of ointment*)


MAGDALENE: Welcome, my lovely Lord, I kneel.
Welcome, my heart, who comest to heal.
Welcome, all my world's weal,
My love and all my bliss.
From thee, Lord, may I not conceal
My filth and my faults so real.
Forgive me that my flesh so frail
To thee hath done amiss.


Ointment here have I ready
To anoint thy sweet body;
Though I be wretch unworthy
Wave me not from thy side.
Full of sin and sorrow am I,
But therefore, Lord, I am sorry;
Amend me through thy great mercy
Be to me my great guide.

> (*She anoints him with tears and ointment and dries his feet with her hair*)

SIMON: Ah, Judas, why does Jesus so?
   Methinks he should let her go,
   This woman of great sin and woe,
   For fear of the world's shame.
   And if he true prophet were,
   He should know her life here
   And suffer her not to come him near
   For the sake of His fame.

JUDAS: Nay, Simon, brother, sooth to say,
   It is nothing for my pay.
   This ointment goes so fast away
   That is of great price.
   This same box might have been sold
   For three hundred pennies told
   And given to the poor of the fold:
   Would be indeed my advice.

MAGDALENE: My Christ, my comfort and my king!
   I worship thee in every thing;
   For now my heart is full loving
   And my thoughts fly above.
   Seven devils now, as I well see
   Thou hast driven out of me,
   Not foul sin but grace to see
   Thou hast led me from love.

JESUS: Peter and Philip, my Brethren free,
   Before you a castle you may see;
   Go you thither and fetch anon to me
   An ass and her foal also.
   Loose them, bring them hither anon.
   If any man stops you as you are gone
   You may say that I will ride thereon
   As soon as they will let them go.

PETER: Master, we shall do your bidding,
   And bring them soon for any thing.
   Philip, brother, let us be going
   To fetch these beasts two.

PHILIP: Brother, I am on the way down;
   Let us hurry to get to the town;
   Great joy let us have at this sound
   Of this errand to do.          (*Exeunt*)

PETER: How, now, I must have this Ass.

   (*All move towards Jerusalem, the citizens strew palms and
     prostrate themselves*)

JESUS: Ha! Jerusalem, holy city.
   Unknown today it is to thee
   What peace thou hast. Canst thou not see?
   Sorrow thou shalt abide.
   Much must thou suffer some day
   When woe shall fall in every way
   And thou shalt be beguiled, truth to say,
   With sorrow on all side.

   Destroyed dolefully, driven down
   No stone standing in this whole town
   Shall be; in the dust lie the crown
   And the men in the tomb.
   And God's own visitation
   Done for mankind's salvation
   Receives no devotion.
   They fear not his doom.      (*Enters the Temple*)

   Go away and do not this thing
   For it is not to my liking.
   You make my father's dwelling
   A place of merchandise.

1ST MERCHANT: What man is this that makes this scare
And casteth down all our ware?
Came no man hither to break and tear
Before our goods to despise.

2ND MERCHANT: Out, out! woe is me!
My table with my money
Is spread abroad, too well I see
And naught dare I say.
Now it seems well that he
Would achieve royalty;
Else thus bold durst he not be
To make such assay.

1ST MERCHANT: It seems well he would be king
Who would cast out our ring
And say his father's dwelling
In this Temple is.
Say, Jesus, with thy jangling,
What evidence or tokening
Showest thou of thy reigning
That thou darest now do this?

2ND MERCHANT: What signs showest thou here
That thou hast such power
To break our ware in this manner
So great in might and main?

JESUS: This Temple here I may destroy
And through my might and my mastery
In days three it re-edify
To build it up again.

1ST MERCHANT: Ah, ha, Jesus, wilt thou so?
This word, as I hope to go,
Shall be repeated so,
And Caiaphas I shall tell.

(JESUS *drives them out with a whip*)

JESUS: Hie you fast from the Temple so,
 No merchandise shall be here, no,
 Not in this place. This shall ye know.
 Here ye shall no longer dwell.

JUDAS: By dear God in majesty
 I am as angry as can be,
 And some way I will revenged be
 As soon as ever I may.
 My master Jesus as men might see
 Was rubbed head, foot and knee
 With ointment far more dainty
 Than I saw for many a day.
 Of that I have great envy
 That he allowed to destroy
 More than all his goods by three
 And his dame's too.
 If I had of it had mastery
 I would have sold it soon full high
 And put it in our treasury
 As I was wont to do.

 Sir Caiaphas and his company
 Conspire Jesu to annoy;
 Their speech anon I will espy
 With falsehood to smear him.
 And if they gladly will know why!
 I shall teach them to draw nigh
 For of his counsel well know I:
 I may best betray him.      (*Exit*)

CAIAPHAS: Lordings, followers of the law,
 Hearken thither to this saw:
 Jesus to him all men can draw,
 All men from all the race.
 If we let him long go on
 All men will believe him upon;

So shall the Romans come anon
And deprive us of our place.
Therefore it is fully in my head
That we find out how he may be dead;
For if long his life be led
Our law goes all to naught.
Therefore say each one his counsel
What manner and way will best avail
This shrew for to assail;
Some trick now must be sought.

ANNAS: Sir, you say right skilfully,
But surely men must espy
From him we take no villainy,
Nor do we dare to fail,
For you know as well as I
Oft have we planned him to try
But he ever hath had the victory;
That no way may avail.

1ST PHARISEE: Yea, sir, in Temple hath he been
And troubled us with ruin;
But when we did hope and ween
Of him to have our will
Wherever we went he slipped away,
Thus making the people in good fay
To believe that he is the Christ verray
Come here our law to spill.

2ND PHARISEE: Yea, Lords, one point should now be ta'en
That Lord Lazarus seemed as slain,
Yet he raised him up again
That four days had been dead.
For that miracle, for his great main,
To honour him they all are fain
And Lazar that dead was will not be lain.
In him a new life is led.

1ST PHARISEE: Lordlings, there is no more to say
But lost is our law, I dare lay,
And he comes on our sabbath day
That now approaches night.
If he heal any, less or more,
All men will believe in his lore
Therefore it is good to slay him before,
If we can be so sly.

JUDAS: Lords, what will you give me
If I shall help that he
Slyly shall betrayed be
Just as you will?

CAIAPHAS: Welcome, fellow, that shall ye do,
That bargain I would keep to you.

JUDAS: Let me see what you will do
And lay down silver here;
For the devil shall call me a liar
If I do it without hire
Either for sovereign or sire.
It is not my manner.

CAIAPHAS: Say on, what we shall give thee
To see that he taken be,
And here is ready thy money
To pay thee before thou pass.

JUDAS: As ever I hope my joy to see,
Or I shall ever show any subtlety,
Thirty pence you shall give me
And not a farthing less.

1ST PHARISEE: Yea, but thy troth thou must plight
To serve us aright,
To betray thy master with all thy might
To earn here thy money.

JUDAS: Have here my troth, as I hold this tight,
  On Friday in the morning or night
  I shall bring him into your sight
  And tell you which is he.

1ST PHARISEE: You are all brethren in a row
  Which is he I do not know.

JUDAS: Now a very sign I shall you show:
  Watch out whom I kiss.
  And that is he, truth to say
  Take him by force as you may
  And lead him slyly away
  Wherever your plan is.

CAIAPHAS: Now look thou serve us truly
  Thy master's coming to espy.

JUDAS: Trust well thereto and truthfully
  He shall not escape.

  On Friday in the morning
  All wait upon my coming,
  For wherever he is walking
  I shall go espy.
  With him I mean to eat and drink,
  And after tidings to you to bring
  Where he intends for his dwelling
  And to tell you I will hie.

END OF ELEVENTH PLAY

12.  THE BETRAYAL OF CHRIST

JESUS: Brethren all, to me right dear,
　　Come hither to me and you shall hear:
　　The feast of Easter you know draws near
　　And now it is at hand.
　　That feast needs keep must we
　　With very great solemnity;
　　The Paschal Lamb eaten must be
　　As the Law doth command.
　　Therefore Peter, look that thou go
　　And John with thee shall be also;
　　Prepare all things that belong thereto
　　According to the Law.


PETER: Lord, thy bidding do will we;
　　But tell us first where it shall be,
　　And we shall do it speedily
　　And thither will we draw.


JESUS: Go into the city which you do see
　　And there a man meet shall ye,
　　A water-pot along beareth he
　　For so you may him know.
　　Into what house that he shall go
　　Into the same house enter you also
　　And say: " The master to thee us sent."
　　To have a place convenient,
　　The Paschal Lamb to eat there is my intent
　　With my disciples all.


　　A fair parlour he will show you;
　　There prepare all things due,
　　Where I and my retinue
　　Fulfill the law we shall.

PETER: All ready, Lord, this thy will
   Shortly we two shall fulfil.
   Our journey we shall go until
   We find that house today.

   (PETER *and* JOHN *go to meet a servant with a water-pot*)


   All hail, good fellow, heartily,
   To thy master's house, we pray thee
   To take us in your company
   Our message for to say.


SERVANT: Come on your way and follow me,
   My master's house you soon shall see.
   For here it lies, truly.
   Say now what you will.                    (*They enter the house*)


PETER: Sir, the Master saluteth thee!
   And as messengers sent are we,
   Wherefore we pray you heartily
   To listen to His will.
   The Master hath sent us to thee;
   A place prepare for Him must we,
   The Paschal Lamb there eat will He
   With His disciples all.


LORD: Lo, here a parlour all ready dight
   With paved floors and windows bright.
   Make all things ready as you think right;
   This chamber have you shall.


JOHN: Now, brother Peter, speedy let us be
   The Paschal Lamb to make ready;
   Then back to our Master you and I
   As fast as ever we may.          (*The Table is prepared*)

PETER: Thy commandment, Lord, done have we;
   The Paschal Lamb is made ready.
   Therefore come on and you shall see
   And we shall lead the way.          (JESUS *enters and sits*)


JESUS: Now, brethren, go to your seat;
   This Paschal Lamb now let us eat,
   Then shall we of other things treat
   That be of great effect.
   For know you now the time is come
   That signs and shadows be all done;
   Therefore make haste that we may soon
   All symbols clean reject.

   For a new law I will begin,
   To help mankind out of his sin,
   So that he may Heaven win
   Which he for sin has lost.
   And here in presence of you all
   Another sacrifice begin I shall
   To save mankind from his sins all,
   For help him I needs must.          (JESUS *reclines*)

   Brethren, I tell you if you draw nigh
   What great desire here have I
   This passover to eat with you truly
   Before my passion.
   Behold I say that you may see
   My father's will, almighty,
   Which I must accept meekly
   In this same fashion.          (JESUS *blesses and breaks bread*)

   This bread I give here my blessing.
   Take ye and eat at my bidding
   For you must be always believing
   This is my body.

That shall do for all mankind
In remission of their sin.
This I give you to bear in mind.
Me after and evermore.

(*He raises the chalice*)

Father of Heaven, I thank thee
For all that Thou hast done for me.
Brethren, take this with heart free
For it is my blood.
It shall be shed upon the tree,
For more together drink never we
Until in heavenly bliss we be
To taste this ghostly food.

Brethren, forsooth, I you say,
One of you shall me betray
That eateth here with me today
In this company.

JAMES: Sorrowful for these words are we;
Who it is I cannot see.
If this lot shall fall to me,
Lord, tell if it be I.

(JUDAS *dips his hand into a cup*)

JESUS: Through his deceit I am all but dead
That in my cup now wets his bread:
Much woe will fall upon his head,
That wretch shall perish, I wis.
Good were it he had not been born
For his body and soul are both forlorn
That so falsely hath against me sworn,
And yet all willed is this.

JUDAS: Dear master, is it not I
That shall do thee this villainy?

JESUS: Thou hast said, Judas, readily,
   For truly thou art he.
   What thou shalt do, do hastily.

JUDAS: Farewell, all this company;
   For on an errand I must hie,
   Undone it may not be.

JESUS: Brethren, take up this meat anon,
   To another task we must soon be gone;
   Your feet shall washed be each one
   To show all charity.
   And first myself I will begin
   And wash all that are herein
   To leave behind no stains of sin,
   And meeker now to be.

PETER: Ah, Lord, shalt thou wash my feet?

JESUS: That I do, Peter, a truth to show;
   In later time more shalt thou know.

PETER: Nay, Lord, forsooth in no manner
   My feet shalt thou wash here.

JESUS: Unless I wash thee, it must be clear,
   Of joy thou gettest no part.

(JESUS *washes their feet*)

JESUS: My dear brethren, well know ye,
   That Lord and Master you call me,
   And right you say, as it should be,
   I am and have been of yore.
   Since I have washed your feet here,
   Lord and Master, in meek manner,
   Do then, each one to other in fear
   As I have done before.

My children and brethren free,
A little while I may with you be,
But thither you go not with me,
As I am now on my way.
But this is truly my bidding:
Love each other in every thing
As I before, without flinching,
Have loved you truly aye.

So all men may know and see
My disciples that you be,
Falsehood if you always flee
And love well together.

PETER: Lord, whither art thou on the way?

JESUS: You will not follow along today
To that place which lies in my way,
Not now, in no manner.
But thou shalt thither go.

PETER: Why shall it not, Lord, now be so?
My life is now put deep in woe
I will for thee be slain.

JESUS: Brethren, let not your hearts be sore,
Believe in God for evermore,
And in Me as you have before,
And moan not for this case.
For in my Father's house there is
Many a mansion of great bliss;
Thither I will go now, I wis,
To prepare for you a place.
And though I go from you away
To find a place to be your pay
I shall come again another day
And take you all with me.

THOMAS: Lord, we know not, in good fay,
    What manner of road thou dost assay;
    Tell us that we know may
    That road and go with Thee.

JESUS: I tell thee, make now no strife,
    In me is the way, the truth and life
    And to my Father, no man nor wife
    May come without Me.
    And if you know me verily
    My Father you may know on high;
    From hence I tell you truly
    Know Him shall all ye.

PHILIP: Lord, let us see they Father anon
    And that will suffice us everyone.

JESUS: A long time you have with me gone;
    Philip, why sayest thou so?
    Truly, he who seeth me
    Seeth my Father, I tell it thee;
    Why wilt thou my Father now see
    While I do with you go?
    Though I go now to distress
    I will not leave you comfortless;
    Believe it well, as I this express,
    Soon I will come again.
    And then your hearts, believe it so,
    Will gladly come my bliss to know,
    A joy which no man can take from you
    Though he were full fain.

    Rise up, and let us go hence anon;
    To prayer I must now be gone,
    But sit you still everyone
    While my Father I do call.     *(He prays and they sleep)*

Wake and take my benison
To keep you from temptation.
The spirit here is willing
But flesh is ready to fall.

Father of Heaven in majesty
Glorify, if thy will it be,
Thy son that He may glorify Thee
Now before from earth I wend.

You sleep, brethren still, I see.
Sleep on then, all ye.
My time is come, taken to be;
From you I must away.
He that hath betrayed me
This night from him I will not flee,
In sorry hour born was he,
And so he may well say.

(JUDAS *arrives with soldiers*)

You men, I ask: whom seek ye?

MALCHUS: Jesus of Nazareth; Him seek we.

JESUS: Here, all ready; I am He.
What have you now to say?

JUDAS: Ah, sweet Master, kiss me,
For it is long since I saw Thee;
Come, together we will flee
And steal from them away.

JESUS: I said before; again I say.
I am he, and, in good fay,
Suffer these men to go their way
For I am at your will.

MALCHUS: False thief! thou shalt be gone
    To Bishop Caiaphas and that anon
    Or I shall break thy body and bone
    If thou durst be late.                    (*A struggle*)

PETER: Thief, how are you so bold
    My Master so roughly to hold.
    Thou shalt be quit a hundredfold,
    And more.  Now I tell you, remember that.
    Be thou so bold, now say I,
    To take my Master and Him to tie
    Full dear for it shalt thou buy.
    Prepare now for Heaven bright!
    Thy ear shall off, by God's grace
    Ere thou passest from this place          (*Cuts off his ear*)
    Go, complain now to Caiaphas
    And bid him make thee right.

MALCHUS: Oh, alas, horror, alas;
    By God's bones, mine ear he has.
    This is for me a dreadful case.
    Woe that I ever came out.

JESUS: Peter, put up thy sword, say I
    Whosoever with sword smiteth gladly
    With that same sword shall perish thereby.
    I tell thee this without doubt.            (*Restores the ear*)

MALCHUS: Ah, well is me!  Oh, well is me!
    My ear is healed, that I do see.
    So merciful a man as he
    Knew I never none.

1ST JEW: Yea, though he had healed thee,
    Saved by us he shall not be.
    But off to Sir Caiaphas must he
    With us he must be gone.

JESUS: As to a thief you come here,
   With swords and staves draw near,
   To take me in foul manner
   And wreak your wicked will.
   In the temple I was with you aye
   Then on me no hand would you lay;
   But now is come that time and day
   Your desires to fulfil.

1ST JEW: Come, caitiff, to Caiaphas,
   Or thou shalt have little grace;
   Trot more swift than this dull pace,
   And hurry now from this ground.
   Though Beelzebub and devil's mate
   Come to thy help, it is thy fate
   To have thy hands bound in this state
   And marched most swiftly round.

END OF TWELFTH PLAY

# PART IV

### 13. CHRIST'S PASSION

1ST JEW: Sir Bishops, here we have brought
 A wretch that much woe hath wrought
 And would bring our law to naught,
 For it he hath spurned.

2ND JEW: Yea, all over we have him sought
 And dearly we have him bought,
 For here many men's thought
 To him he hath turned.

ANNAS: Ah, jangling Jesu, art thou here?
 Now mayst thou prove thy power
 Whether thy cause be clean and clear,
 Thy Christhood we shall know.

CAIAPHAS: Methinks a master, if he were
 Either by pennies or by prayer,
 Might shift away this great danger
 And much great skill would show.

ANNAS: Sir Caiaphas, I tell thee truly
 That all of us in this company
 Must needs this smart fellow destroy
 That wickedly hath wrought.

CAIAPHAS: It is needful, this say I
 That one must die, verily,
 All men's souls to buy
 So that they perish not.

1ST JEW: Sir Caiaphas, hearken now to me,
   This babbler our King would be,
   Whatever he says now before thee
   I heard him say before.
   That prince he was of such degree
   Destroy the Temple well might he
   And build it up within days three
   As it was in days of yore.

2ND JEW: Yes, truly, I heard him say,
   He may deny it in no way,
   That he was the God verray,
   Emmanuel and Messiah.
   He may not deny this in any way
   For more than twenty, in good fay,
   That in the Temple were that day
   Heard the words of this liar.

JESUS: As thou sayest, so say I.
   I am God's son almighty:
   And here I tell thee truly
   That me yet shalt thou see
   Sit on God's hand, Him by
   Mankind in cloud to justify,

ALL: Witness all this company
   That falsely lieth he.

CAIAPHAS: You hearken to all he sayeth here!
   What need of witness were there
   When, before all these folk, together,
   Loudly, thy voice lies?
   What say you, men standing here?

1ST JEW: Buffets for this behaviour,
   A new law we shall make him fear
   That our law so destroys.

For his harms here
Now I will come near,
For his strong jeer
That makes our law false.


2ND JEW: He is, have no fear,
To the devil most dear.
Spit we and leer
And buffet till he falls.


1ST JEW: Fie on thee, fellow!
Now you may look meek.
Thy bones I will break,
I am ready now.


His face will I hide.
Now if he cried
Who smote his side
He is the Christ.


2ND JEW: For all he prophesies,
If he fails thrice
My stick at him flies,
He gets my hard fist.


1ST JEW: And more if I may
I shall soon assay.
You shall for it pay,
Thou prince, on thy pate.


2ND JEW: And if he say nay,
I shall, by my fay,
Do as I say
It is not too late.

CAIAPHAS: Lordings, what shall be said?
   This man deserves to be dead
   And if for this he is lightly led
   Our law will be asleep.

ANNAS: Sir, it is my best advice
   That he is led to justice
   To Sir Pilate, so wary and wise,
   Who has the law to keep.       (*Thy take him to* PILATE)

CAIAPHAS: Sir Pilate, here we bring one
   Who hath our Elders' law misdone
   And says tribute may be given none
   To Caesar, and his power.
   Wheresoever he and his fellows have gone
   They turn folk to their ways anon;
   Now we demand justice him upon
   From thee at this hour.

ANNAS: Indeed he is our Elders' foe;
   Wheresoever he goeth to and fro,
   Claiming to be King and Christ also
   He causes all annoy.
   Knew Caesar that, he would rave so
   If such a man we here let go.
   Therefore judge him to woe
   Lest he us all destroy.

PILATE: What sayest thou, man in disarray?
   If thou art the King of Jews now say.

JESUS: As thou hast said, men have heard say.
   A King that shall all amaze.

PILATE: No cause, find I, in good fay,
   To do this man to death today.

CAIAPHAS: Sir, the people follow his way.
  Perverted them all he has.

PILATE: Fault in him can I find none.
  Therefore it is best that we let him be gone
  And out of these doors let him go yon
  Whither he will to take his way.

1ST JEW: Nail him, we cry aloud with one voice.
  Nail him, nail him to a cross.

PILATE: You men, for shame!  Make still your noise!
  My counsel will I say.
  You know, everyone standing here,
  That I must release to you a prisoner,
  For the feast approaches near
  All in honour of that day.
  Will you Jesus delivered see?

2ND JEW: Nay, to suffer death worthy is he.
  And to that, cry out all we
  That " Barabbas be saved ".

PILATE: What shall I do with this same Jesus here,
  That Christ is called and held in fear?

1ST JEW: Nail him on cross in any manner
  For that he hath deserved.

PILATE: Now since I see you so fervent
  And set that his life shall be rent,
  Wash will I here, all you present
  Rage however you should.   (*He washes his hands before them*)
  You all shall know this intent
  That I am clean and innocent.
  By washing my hands all this is meant.
  I am free of this man's blood.                (*To* JESUS)

Men of thine own nation
Call for thy Damnation
With many an accusation
Before me here today.
Art thou king, as they all cry?

JESUS: My realm is not, thus say I,
Of this world, but if it were, truly
With Jews should I not take my way:
And if my realm of this world were,
Strive with you I would now here
And thrust off with such power
To deprive you of your prey.
But my might in this manner
I shall not prove, not shall appear
Like a worldly king, with cause unclear,
As if in good fay.

PILATE: Ergo a king thou art or wast.

JESUS: As thou sayest, it is no less;
But now I tell thee express
That King I am and may be.
To the world I came to bear witness
Of kindness, therefore born I was
And all that live in soothness
My glory hereafter shall see.

PILATE: What is soothness, tell thou me.

JESUS: Soothness comes from God's own see.

PILATE: In earth then this truth cannot be?

JESUS: How can truth live in earth, tell me?
When misjudged on earth is he
Who has over all high authority?

PILATE: Lord, I find no cause can be
    To condemn this man before me.


1ST JEW: Come now, with care,
    Hard shalt thou fare
    On thy body bare
    Strokes shalt thou bear.


2ND JEW: In woe shall he be wounded
    And to grains grounded
    No lad up in London
    Can find such good law there.

    (*They strip and beat him and dress him in purple robes*)


1ST JEW: Now since he King is
    Right his clothing is.
    Of thorns this thing is
    Just for him to wear.

                            (*Crown of thorns added*)


2ND JEW: Now to thy crown of weed
    Add here a reed.
    Sceptre thou shalt need
    A king for to be.


1ST JEW: Hail, King of Jews
    Whom so many shrews
    With ribald ruse
    Do thee reverence.              (*They kneel before* JESUS)


2ND JEW: With spittle and spew
    With scourge we shall hew,
    Anointing thy brow
    For this thine offence.

PILATE: Lordings, here you may see
  Your king in his majesty.

CAIAPHAS: Nay, sir, forsooth no King have we
  Save the Emperor of Rome.
  But nail him to the tree
  Or the Emperor full wroth will be.

ANNAS: What we say is as sayeth he:
  Pass on him now his doom.

PILATE: Which of the two shall I release,
  Jesus Christ or Barabbas?

CAIAPHAS: Sure Jesu, thou traitor to our peace,
  Must be nailed upon the tree,
  And let Barabbas go his way.

PILATE: Take him forth then, as you say;
  For save him now I never may,
  Though undone I should be.

IST JEW: This judgement is at an end;
  Now I suggest that we should wend
  This shrew to his death to send
  A little here beside.

(*They move to Calvary*)

ANNAS: He seems weary of his way;
  Some help to get I will assay,
  For this cross, in good fay,
  So far he cannot bear.
  Simon, here, from Cyrene
  Take this cross, I command thee
  And to the mount of Calvary
  Help that it should be borne.

SIMON: To bear no cross is my intent
    For it was never my assent
    To procure this prophet's judgement,
    Who is full of the Holy Ghost.

CAIAPHAS: Simon, thou to prison will be sent
    To suffer pain and punishment;
    This cross for thy back is meant
    Cease now all this vain boast.

SIMON: Alas, that ever I did hither come!
    Would to God I were still at Rome,
    Why did I cross the ocean's foam
    Thus to be annoyed?
    But, Lord, I take thee to witness
    That I do this at my distress.
    All Jews for this falseness
    I hope will be destroyed.        *(He takes the cross)*

CAIAPHAS: Hurry forth, or 'twill be night.
    Strip him, now, who has done us spite.

1ST JEW: This coat shall be mine
    For it is good and fine
    And seam there is none within
    That I can see.

2ND JEW: Nay, friend, by my fay,
    At the dice we shall play
    Thus shall we say
    Who this weed shall win.        *(They strip JESUS)*

1ST JEW: Fellow, let's see
    Here are dice three,
    Which shall it be
    Shall win this ware?

Now will I begin
To cast my dice in,
This coat for to win,
This is good and rare.                    *(Casts dice)*
As I have good grace
Won it thou hast;
It stares in the face
You are winner there.


CAIAPHAS: Men, for Godsake, make haste
How long shall this wheyface
Stand naked in this place?
Go, nail him to the tree!


1ST JEW: Anon, master, anon.
A hammer have I one.


2ND JEW: And nails to fasten on
Though he were my brother.


1ST JEW: Here is a rope will last
To strengthen this mast.


2ND JEW: On this cross now to cast
And here pull another.


1ST JEW: Draw tight for your father's kin
While I now drive in
This long iron pin
In his hands it will stay.


2ND JEW: Now, by this light
His feet place thou right
For my troth now I plight
He will stand well today.

*(They raise* CHRIST *up on the cross)*

PILATE: Come hither, thou, I command thee!
　Go, nail this tablet on the tree;
　Since he King of the Jews will be
　He must have recognition.
　" Jesu of Nazareth ", men may see
　" King of Jews ", how like ye?
　I wrote thereon, as said he,
　For this was his mission.

2ND JEW: Now, Sir Pilate, to us take heed,
　King is he not, so God me speed!
　Therefore thou dost a sorry deed;
　Such writing everyone rues.
　Thou shouldst write that many might read,
　How he lied here indeed
　And told all without need
　That he was King of the Jews.

PILATE: What I have written, I have written.
　　　　　　　(*They look to the cross and* MARY *enters*)

MARY: Alas, my love, my life, what do I see?
　Alas, this mourning has maddened me.
　Alas! my comfort look thou be
　To thy mother that thee bore.
　Think of my fright! I that fostered thee
　And gave thee to suck upon my knee!
　Upon my pain have now pity;
　Thou hast in earth all power.
　Alas, the sorrow of this sight
　Mars my mind, main and might,
　But still my heart me thinks is light
　To look on him that I love.
　And when I look anon right
　Upon my child for whom I could fight
　I would Death deliver me this night
　Then should we meet above.

JESUS: Father of Heaven, if thy will be
 Forgive them for what they have done to me!
 For they are all blind and may not see
 How foully they do amiss.

CAIAPHAS: If thou art so great and mighty,
 God's true son in majesty,
 Come down and we will believe in thee
 That truly so it is.

MARY: Alas, my heart will break in three.
 Alas, Death, I conjure thee,
 My life, son, thou take from me
 To separate me from woe.

JESUS: Eli, eli, eli, eli!
 My God my God, I speak to thee!
 Eli, lama sabachthani?
 Why hast thou forsaken me?

1ST JEW: Ah, hark! he calls upon Eli
 For to deliver him hastily.

2ND JEW: Abide and we shall soon see
 Whether Eli dare come here or no.

JESUS: My thirst is sore, my thirst is sore.

1ST JEW: Yea, thou shalt have a drink therefore.
 That thou shalt like to drink no more
 Of all this seven year.

JESUS: Almighty God in majesty,
 To work thy will I am resigned;
 My spirit I commend to thee
 Receive it, Lord, into thy hand.   (*He* dies)

PILATE: Joseph, I tell without nay,
That body thou shalt have today;
But let me know, I thee pray,
Whether his life be gone.
Hark, Jew, is Jesus dead?

2ND JEW: Yea, Sir, as ever break I bread,
In him is no life led,
Nor never a whole vein.

PILATE: Joseph, then take him to thee;
Go now and let him buried be;
But look thou makest no sorcery
To raise him up again.                    (JESUS *is taken down*)

JOSEPH OF ARIMATHEA: Grant you mercy, Sir, of dignity!
You need not warn this to me,
For rise again I know will he
By his own might and main.                 (*exit* PILATE)

Now the sun has lost his light,
Earthquakes make men affright,
The rock all firm upon the height
Cleaves open that men may know.
Sepulchres open in men's sight;
Dead men rise during this sad night,
To say that he is God Almight
Who such signs to men can show.
Therefore brought here have I
A hundred pounds of spicery,
Myrrh, aloes and many more thereby
To honour him will I bring;
For to embalm his sweet body,
In this sepulchre to lie,
That he may have on me mercy,
When in Heaven he is King.

END OF THIRTEENTH PLAY

### 14.   CHRIST'S RESURRECTION

CAIAPHAS: And this was yesterday about noon?

PILATE: Yea, Sir Bishop, then 'twas done.
　　Such terrors by day I have seen none,
　　When I let them bury him soon
　　In a tomb of stone.
　　And, therefore, sirs, amongst us three
　　Let us ordain and oversee
　　Lest any peril there be
　　Before we have left and gone.

CAIAPHAS: Sir Pilate, all this was done
　　As we saw after soon,
　　But, believe, by afternoon
　　The weather began to clear.
　　And, Sir, if it be your will
　　Such words you keep still
　　Lest the people may hear.

ANNAS: Yea, Sir Pilate, this say I
　　I saw him and his company
　　Raise men with sorcery
　　That long before were dead.
　　For if there be any more witchcraft
　　That may be done by those that are left
　　His body may soon be from us reft,
　　So consider what shall be said.

CAIAPHAS: Yea, Sir Pilate, I tell thee right,
　　Let us ordain many a hard knight,
　　Well armed, to stand and fight
　　With power and force.
　　That no shame to us befall
　　Let us order here among us all

Some true men to us call
To keep well the corse.

PILATE: Now, by Jesus that died on the rood
Methinks your counsel is wondrous good;
The best men of kin and blood
Anon I will call in.
Sir Colphran and Sir Jerafas
also with Sir Gerapas!
We pray you, sirs, here in this case
To see that you are smart.
Forsooth this I heard him say
That he would rise the third day;
Now, surely, if he may
We shall be there, take heart.

1ST SOLDIER: Yea, let him rise if he dare
If I'm there, let him beware,
I shall deal with him there
He will not get away.

2ND SOLDIER: If he once do heave up his head,
And I do not leave him soon dead
I shall never more eat bread
Nor ever more be at peace.

3RD SOLDIER: Have good day, sirs! We will be gone.
Give us our charge, every one.

CAIAPHAS: Now farewell, best of blood and bone,
Now take heed unto my law.
For as I am a true Jew,
If now any treason ensue
I tell you that you shall all rue
And to death each I shall draw.

(THE SOLDIERS *walk to tomb*)

1ST SOLDIER: The tomb is here at our hand
  Set us now as we shall stand.
  If he dares rise we shall all band
  To beat him all adown.

2ND SOLDIER: Stand thou here and thou there
  And I myself the middle shall bear.
  I trow our hearts shall show no fear
  For they are all stoutly set.

  (ANGELS *sing and* JESUS *rises from tomb*)

JESUS: Earthly man, whom I have wrought
  Awake out of thy sleep!
  Earthly man, whom I have bought
  Of me thou takest no keep.
  From Heaven man's soul I sought
  In a dark dungeon deep;
  My faithful souls from thence I brought
  In pity for them I weep.
  I am very Prince of peace
  And King of free mercy;
  Who will of sins have release
  On me let him call and cry.
  And if he will of sins once cease
  I grant them peace truly
  And thereto a full rich mass
  Of bread, my own body.
  I am very bread of life
  From Heaven I step and send
  Who eateth this bread, man or wife,
  Shall live with me without end.

  (JESUS *departs*: *two* ANGELS *appear*)

1ST SOLDIER: Out, alas, where am I?
  So bright it is hereby
  That my heart wholly
  Out of darkness is shaken.

2ND SOLDIER: Where are you, oh comrade dear?
    About me is wondrous clear.
    My heart is caught in a dreadful fear
    And heaved right out of my breast.


3RD SOLDIER: Alas, what is this great light
    Shining here in my sight?
    Marred I am in main and might,
    To move I have no means.


1ST SOLDIER: Yea, we are all taken surely.
    For Jesu is risen, that know I
    Out of the sepulchre mightily;
    The sight of it I have in mind.


2ND SOLDIER: In a wicked time had we
    Nailed him on the Rood Tree
    For as he said, in days three
    Risen he is and gone.


3RD SOLDIER: I will to Caiaphas, by my fay,
    The truth openly to say.
    Farewell, sirs, and have good day!
    Jesu Master is and more.

                (*Exeunt*, the *three* MARIES *enter*)


MARY MAGDALENE: Alas, now lost is all my liking,
    For woe I wander and hands do wring;
    My heart in sorrow and sighing
    Is sadly set and sore.
    He I most loved of all thing,
    Alas, is now full low lying.
    Why, Lord, am I still living
    To tell all this lonesome lore?

MARY JACOBI: Alas, wellaway, my sorrows are all pent
My help and healing are spent;
My Christ, my only comfort, rent
And covered now in clods of clay.
Mighty God omnipotent
Give them hard judgement
That his body so twisted and bent,
For this now, I pray.

MARY SALOME: Alas, now marred is all my might,
My Lord through whom my heart was light
So shamefully slain here in my sight;
My sorrow cannot be fought.
Since I may have no other right
From the devils that killed in their spite
I will balm his body that is so bright;
A box with me have I brought.

MARY MAGDALENE: Sister, which of us, each one,
Shall remove this great stone,
That lies my sweet Lord upon?
For move it I never may.

MARY JACOBI: Sister, such power I have none,
It seems to me he were gone
For on the sepulchre there sitteth one
And the stone rolled away.

MARY SALOME: Two children there I see sitting.
All of white is their clothing
And the stone beside lying,
Go we near and see.

IST ANGEL: What seek ye, women, what seek ye here?
With weeping and with great mischeer?

Jesus, that to you was so dear
Is risen, believe you me.

2ND ANGEL: Be not afraid, stand not in fear!
    For he is gone away from here
    He has gone before and near
    Unto Galilee.

MARY MAGDALENE: Ah, hie we fast for any thing
    And tell Peter this tiding;
    A blessedful word we may him bring
    And true let us hope it were.

MARY JACOBI: Yea, walk thou, sister, by one way
    And we two another shall assay
    Till we have met with him today
    My dearest of Lords so fair.
                (MARY JACOBI *and* MARY SALOME *exeunt*)

MARY MAGDALENE: Hence will I never full truly
    Till I be comforted for such a loss as he
    And know where he is readily,
    Here will I sit and weep.

ANGEL: Woman, why weepest thou, say?

MARY MAGDALENE: Son, for that my Lord is taken away
    And I know not at all, sooth to say
    Who hath done this thing.
    Alas, why were I not dead today
    Caught down under the clods of clay
    To see my Lord that here did lay
    Once to my knowing?

JESUS: Woman, why weepest thou, tell me why?
    Whom seekest thou so tenderly?

MARY MAGDALENE: My Lord, sir, was buried hereby
   And now He is away;
   If thou hast done us this annoy
   Tell me, dear sir, hastily
   At once I beg you say.

JESUS: Woman, is not thy name Mary?

MARY MAGDALENE: Ah, Lord, I ask thee mercy.

JESUS: Mary, touch not my body
   For yet I have not been
   With my Father Almighty:
   But to my brethren do thou hie
   And of this thing thou certify
   That thou hast truly seen.
   Say to them all that I will be gone
   To my Father that I came from,
   For He is their Father also;
   Haste, look thou dost not dwell.

MARY MAGDALENE: Ah, blessed be Thou for ever so!
   Now waived is all my woe.
   With this joy I now must go
   The rest this news to tell.     *(She meets the others)*
   Ah, women, no more to bewail there is;
   My Lord Jesu is risen, I wis,
   With Him a little I spake ere this
   And saw Him with this mine eye.
   My woe is turned into bliss
   Mirth in mind there none shall miss
   For He bade me warn all those of His
   To Heaven that He would fly.

MARY JACOBI: Ah, sister, go we and search and see
   Whether these words the truth may be;

No gladness were half so much to me
As to see him in this place.

MARY SALOME: Ah, sister, I beseech thee
    With great haste let us all three
    For this great joy in speed to see
    And see His fair face.                    (*They are met by* JESUS)

JESUS: All hail, women, all hail!

MARY JACOBI: Ah, Lord, we believe without fail
    That Thou art risen us to heal,
    And deliver us from woe.

MARY SALOME: Ah, welcome be Thou, my own Lord sweet
    Let us kiss Thy blessed feet
    And handle Thy wounds that seem so wet
    Ere we hence may go.

JESUS: Be not afraid, women, of me,
    But to my brethren now wend ye,
    And bid them go to Galilee
    There meet with me they must.

MARY JACOBI: Anon, Lord, done it shall be,
    Well for them this sight to see;
    For mankind, Lord, is bought by Thee.
    In this Thy Passion was just.

MARY SALOME: Peter, tidings good and new!
    We have seen my Lord Jesu,
    Alive and fresh in skin and hue,
    And handled have his feet.

PETER: Well it is, ye have been true,
    But I forswore that I him knew;

Therefore shame makes me eschew
With my Lord to meet.
But yet I hope to see His face
In spite of my so great trespass;
My sorrow of heart well known He has
And of it will take heed.
In that place He buried was
I will hie me and run apace
Of my sweet Lord to ask grace
For my foul misdeed.


JESUS: Peter, knowst thou not me?


PETER: Ah, Lord, mercy I ask Thee
With sorry heart, kneeling on my knee;
Forgive me my trespass.
My faint flesh and my frailty
Made me Lord, false to be,
But forgiveness with heart free
Grant me, Lord, through thy grace.


JESUS: Peter as I had foresight
That thou shouldst forsake me that night,
Keep now that deed in sight
When thou sittest in sovereignty.
Think on thy own deed today
That flesh is frail and failing aye,
And be thou merciful alway
As now I am to thee.


Therefore I suffered thee to fall
That to thy subjects, hereafter all
When to thee they shall cry and call
Thy mercy shall then increase.
Since thyself so fallen has

Be more inclined to grant grace.
Go forth, forgiven is thy trespass,
And here now I thee do bless.


END OF FOURTEENTH PLAY


### 15. CHRIST'S ASCENSION

JESUS: My Brethren that sit in company,
I greet you in peace full heartfeltly;
I am He that shall stand by thee:
Fear you for nothing.
Well I know, and that truly,
That you are in great ecstasy
Whether I be risen verily
Which makes you sore in longing.
There is no need to be worried so,
Nor in your minds to be in woe;
Put forth your hands to me so
And feel my wounds so wet;
And believe this, all and one,
That ghosts have neither flesh nor bone,
And that you may feel me upon
My hands and upon my feet.

PETER: Ah, what is this that stands us by?
A Ghost he seems to be verily;
Methinks lightened much am I
This spirit for to see.

ANDREW: Peter, I tell thee secretly,
I dread me yet full greatly
That Jesu should show such mystery
And whether that this be he.

JOHN: Brethren, good is it to think ever more,
　　What words he spake the day before
　　He died on cross, he had not gone for evermore
　　And we should be steadfast aye.

JAMES: Ah, John, that leaves us in fear
　　That he will as he please appear,
　　And when we most wish to have him here
　　Then will he be away.

JESUS: I see well, brethren, sooth to say,
　　Despite any sign that I display,
　　Ye are not steadfast in your fay
　　For flinching I you find.
　　More signs therefore ye shall see.
　　Have you aught may eaten be?

PETER: Yea, Lord, meat enough for Thee,
　　Or else we were unkind.

JESUS: Now eat we then in charity,
　　My dear brethren, fair and free,
　　For all things shall fulfilled be
　　Written in Moses' law.
　　Prophets in psalms said of Me
　　That death awaited Me on the rood tree,
　　To rise within days three
　　To joy mankind to draw.
　　And preach to folk this world within
　　Penance and remission of their sin;
　　In Jerusalem I should begin
　　As I have done for love.
　　Therefore believe steadfastly
　　And come with Me to Bethany.
　　In Jerusalem you shall all be
　　To await the grace from above.

*(They eat together)*

My sweet brethren, dearest so dear,
To Me is granted fullest power
In Heaven and earth, both far and near,
For My Godhead is most.
To teach all men now go ye,
That in the world will followed be,
In the name of My father and of Me
And of the Holy Ghost.

> (*Sings*) Ascendo ad Patrem meum et Patrem vestrum,
> Deum meum et Deum vestrum: Alleluia!
>
> (*He ascends and the* ANGELS *sing*)

1ST ANGEL: Who is this that cometh within?
  The bliss of Heaven ne'er so great hath been;
  Souls out of the world of sin
  And out of the grip of hell hath He.

2ND ANGEL: Comely He is in His clothing,
  Who with full power is going;
  A number of saints with him leading
  So powerful and great is He.

JESUS: I that speak righteousness
  Have brought man out of distress;
  For Buyer I am called and was
  Of all mankind through grace.
  My people that were from Me reft
  Through sin and through the devil's craft
  To heaven I bring and not one left
  All that in Hell there was.

3RD ANGEL: Why is thy body now so red?
  Thy body is bloody and thy head?
  Thy clothes are they which fit the dead
  And stained as with red wine.

JESUS: These drops now, with good intent,
   To my Father I will present
   That good men that to earth be lent
   Shall know certainly,
   How graciously that I them bought
   And for good works that they wrought
   The everlasting bliss they have sought
   I proved the good worthy.
   For this cause, believe you Me,
   The drops I shed on the rood tree
   All fresh shall reserved be
   Ever till the last day.

     (*He ascends and* ANGELS *descend to apostles singing:* " Viri
       Galilei quid aspicitis in coelum? ")

1ST ANGEL: You men that be of Galilee,
   Whereupon now wonder ye,

2ND ANGEL: Right so again come shall he
   Even as you saw him go.

PETER: Lo, brethren what the Angels maintain,
   That Jesus, who through His great main,
   To Heaven is gone, will come again
   Just as He went forth.

ANDREW: Many times so promised He
   To send His spirit with strength so free
   And in Jerusalem we should be
   Till He is to us sent.

PETER: Go we, brethren, with one assent
   And fulfil His commandment;
   But look that none in dread be pent
   But believe all steadfastly.

Pray we all, with full intent
That he to us his power will send.
Jesus, that from us now went
Save all this company.  Amen.


END OF FIFTEENTH PLAY

## PART V

16. ANTICHRIST

EXPOSITOR (*carrying the Scriptures*):
  Now fifteen signs, while I have space.
  I shall declare, by God's grace,
  Of which St. Jerome mention makes
  To fall before the day of Doom.
  All which were written upon a row,
  He found in books of Hebrew;
  Now will I tell in words a few
  A while if you will dwell.

  The first days, as I written find,
  The Sea shall rise against mankind,
  And as a wall against the wind,
  Above all hills on high,
  Forty cubits, so read we.
  The second day so low shall be
  That scarcely a man the sea shall see,
  Stand he never so high.

  The Third day after, so read I
  Great fishes above the sea shall lie,
  Yell and roar so hideously
  That only God shall hear.
  The fourth day coming then
  Sea and water against all men
  Shall boil, that all may ken
  The end as though it were.

  The fifth day, so read we,
  All manner of herb and tree

132

Of bloody dew all full shall be,
And man and beast all dazed.
Fowls shall gather them, as I find,
Into the fields, each in his kind,
Of meat and drink shall have no mind
But stand all mad, amazed.

The sixth day in the world over all,
Buildings to ground shall fall:
Church, City, House and wall,
And men in graves shall shake.
Lightning and fire are meant
Down from the sun and firmament
To strike until they are spent
And a terror of night shall make.

The seventh day, both rock and stone
Shall break asund and fight and moan;
The sound thereof shall hear no-one
But only God Almight.
The eighth day, earthquake shall be,
That men and beast—believe you me—
Shall fail to stand or see
But fall to ground in fright.

The ninth day, as our books maintain
Hills shall fall and wax all plain;
Stone turn to sand through God's main,
And close up on men so sad.
The tenth day men out of caves shall flee
In fear such signs to see;
To speak together they are not free
But go as they are mad.

The eleventh day worse shall be seen:
When all graves in the world open have been
The dead shall stand all lank and lean
Above the earth standing.

The twelfth day, stars shall fall from high
And fire shoot from them hideously;
All manner of beasts shall roar and cry
Without eating and drinking.

The thirteenth day, shall die all men
And rise again just then.
The fourteenth day shall burn all men,
The earth and also Heaven.
The fifteenth day, made shall be
New earth, new Heaven for God to see.
In that Heaven God grant us to be
For all his names seven.

Now I have told you in good fay
The tokens to come before Doomsday:
God give you grace to do so aye
That then you worthy be,
To come to the bliss that lasteth aye,
As much as here and in our play
Antichrist's signs you see may
For he comes soon, you shall see.                    (*Exit*)

ANTICHRIST: Of me was spoken in prophecy
By Moses, David and Isay;
I am he they call Messy,
Redeemer of Israel.
Those that believe steadfastly
I shall save and set them free
And such joy as lies in me
I think to them to deal.

But one hath belied me in this land,
Jesu his name, I understand;
Of further falsehood He is fond
And fired with fantasy.

By all his wickedness He did stand
Till He was taken and put in bond
Through the virtue of my hand.
This is so, all truly.

One thing gladdens me, I make bold,
As Daniel the prophet before me told;
All women should love me like gold
When I shall come to the land.
This prophecy I shall well hold,
Which is most likely in young and old:
I think many fast to hold,
And all their fairness in my hand.

Also he told, then believe you me,
That I with gifts should be free,
Which prophecy done shall be,
When I my realm have won.
And that I should grant men mercy,
Plenteous riches, land and fee;
It shall be done, that you shall see,
When hither I am come.

What say you, kings, that here be lent?
Are not my words at your assent
That I am Christ omnipotent,
Believe you not this, each one?

1ST KING: We believe, Lord, without let,
That Christ is not come here yet;
If thou be he, thou shalt be set
In Temple as God alone.

2ND KING: If thou art Christ, called Messy,
That from our woe shall us buy,
Show before us thy mastery
With a sign that we may see.

1st KING: Then will I believe that it is so,
    If thou do wonders ere thou go;
    So that thou save us of our woe,
    Then honoured shalt thou be.

2nd KING: Foul have we lived many a year,
    And in our minds lurks great fear;
    If thou art Christ now come here,
    Then may thou stint all strife.

ANTICHRIST: That I am Christ and Christ will be,
    By very signs you shall see,
    For dead men soon shall be free
    And rise from death to life.
    Now will I overturn through my might,
    Trees down with roots upright;
    That is a marvel to your sight,
    And fruit growing upon.
    So shall they grow and multiply
    Through my might and mastery;
    I lead you out of heresy
    To believe me upon.

    And bodies that are dead and slain,
    If I can raise them up again,
    Shall honour me with might and main;
    Then shall no man grieve.
    Forsooth then after will I die
    And rise again and stand on high;
    If I may do this marvellously
    I make you in me to believe.

    Men buried in graves, as you may see,
    What mastery is this, think ye,
    To raise them up and make them free,
    And all through my accord?

Whether I in my godhead be,
By a true sign you shall see.
Rise up, dead men, and honour me,
And know me for your Lord.

*(The dead arise from sepulchres)*

1ST DEAD MAN: Ah, Lord, of thee I ask mercy,
I was dead, but I live and see;
Now I know well and truly
That Christ is hither come.

2ND DEAD MAN: Him honour all men and we,
Devoutly kneeling on our knee,
To worship thee, so shall it be.
Christ calls and we come.

ANTICHRIST: That I shall fulfil holy writ
You shall learn and know of it,
For I am the well of all man's wit
And lord of every land.
And as the prophet Sophony
Speaks of me truthfully
I shall repeat here readily
That clerks shall understand.

Now will I die that you shall see,
And rise again full speedily.
I would in grave that you put me
And worship me alone;
For in this Temple a tomb is made,
Therein my body shall be laid;
Then will I rise, as I have said.
Pay heed to me, each one.

And after my resurrection,
Then will I sit in great renown,
And my ghost send to you down.
I die, I die, now am I dead.

*(Dies)*

1ST KING: Now since this worthy lord is dead,
    And his grace to us is led,
    Take his body as he has said
    And bury it in a grave.

2ND KING: Forsooth, so to us he said,
    In a tomb he would be laid.
    Now go we forth all unafraid;
    From disease he may us save.

1ST KING: Take we the body of this sweet
    And lay it low under the grit.
    Now, Lord, comfort us, this we seek
    And send us of thy grace.

2ND KING: And if he rise through his might,
    From death to life in my sight,
    Him will I honour, day and night
    As God in every place.      *(They leave the tomb)*

1ST KING: Now know I well that he is dead,
    For now in grave we have him laid.
    If he rise as he hath said,
    He is full of great might.

2ND KING: I must mourn with all my main
    Till Christ be risen up again,
    And his miracle here maintain.
    Rise up, Lord, in our sight.      (ANTICHRIST *rises*)

ANTICHRIST: I rise, now, reverence do to me.
    God glorified, greatest of degree.
    If I be Christ, now believe ye me.
    And work as I advise.

1ST KING: Ah, Lord, welcome must thou be
That thou art God, now believe we;
Therefore go, sit in thy see
An accept our sacrifice                    (*They make sacrifices*)

2ND KING: Forsooth in seat thou shalt be set,
And honoured with lamb and goat
As Moses' Law lasteth yet
As he hath said before.

1ST KING: Oh, gracious Lord, go, sit down then!
And we shall both, thy kneeling men
Worship the Christ who is risen
And work after thy lore.

                    (ANTICHRIST *occupies the throne*)

ANTICHRIST: I Lord, I God, I high justice,
I Christ that made the dead to rise,
Here I receive your sacrifice
And bless you, flesh and fell.
You kings, I tell without a boast
I will now send my holy ghost,
To know me lord of might most,
Of heaven, earth and hell.

    (A SPIRIT *is heard saying:* " I shall send you a new heart
        and spirit into your midst ".)

2ND KING: Ah, God, ah, Lord, great of might,
This Holy Ghost hath upon me alight,
Me thinks my heart is very bright,
Since it came into me.

1ST KING: Lord, we honour thee, day and night,
For thou showest us in sight
Just as Moses told aright.
Honoured must thou be!

ANTICHRIST: Yet worthy works to your will
   Of prophecy I shall fulfil
   As before you heard from Daniel
   That lands I should devise.
   That prophecy it shall be done,
   As you see under this sun;
   To worship me as you have begun
   And done as was wise.


   You kings, I shall advance you all
   And because your regions be but small
   Cities and castles shall to you befall
   With towns and towers gay,
   And make you lords of lordships fair,
   As all shall fall from my power;
   Yea, look you do as I you dare
   And hearken what I say.


   I am very god of might,
   All things I made through my might,
   Sun and Moon, Day and Night.
   To bliss I may you bring.
   Therefore kings, noble and gay,
   Token your people what I say,
   That I am Christ, God verray,
   And tell them such tiding.


   My people by Jews were put me from,
   Therefore great pity I have them on;
   If they will believe me upon.
   I shall full soon assay.
   For all that believe me upon
   Worldly wealth shall them fall on,
   And to my bliss they shall come,
   And dwell with me for aye.

2ND KING: Grant mercy, Lord, your gifts today!
  Honour we will thee always;
  Never so rich were we, in good fay,
  Nor none of all our kin.


ANTICHRIST: Therefore be true and steadfast aye,
  Believe in what I say,
  For I will visit on you today,
  And much shall you win.


ENOCH: Almighty God in majesty,
  That made the Heaven and earth to be,
  Fire, water, stone and tree,
  And man through thy might.
  Many points thy secrets be,
  For earthly man to see
  Is impossible, as thinks me,
  For any worldly wight.
  Gracious Lord, that art so good,
  Who so long in flesh and blood
  Hath granted life and Heavenly food,
  Let our thoughts never be defiled.
  But give us, Lord, might and main,
  Or we of this shrew be slain,
  To convert Thy people again
  Whom he hath thus beguiled.


ELIAS: Oh, Lord, that made all thing
  And long hath lent us living,
  Let never the devil's power spring;
  This man hath him within!
  God give you grace, both old and young,
  To know deceit in his doing
  That you may come to that liking
  Of bliss that you may win.

I warn you, all men, fully,
This is Enoch, I am Eli,
We are come his errors to destroy
That he to you now shows.
He calls himself Christ and Messy;
He lies, forsooth, openly.
He is the Devil, you to annoy
And for none other him know.

1st King: Ah, men, what speak you of Eli
And Enoch? They dwell in other company;
Of our blood they are, full truly,
And we are of their kind.

2nd King: We read in books of our law,
That they to Heaven were borne.
Of that there is a common saw
And written men may it find.

Enoch: We are those men, forsooth I wis,
Come to tell you do amiss,
And bring your souls to Heaven's bliss
And these our words to prove.

Elias: This devil's limb that now come is
That says Heaven and earth is his,
Now we are ready—believe this!
Against him for to move.

1st King: If we hear disputation
To support that protestation,
That you have skill and reason
With you we will abide.

2nd King: And if your skills may do him down,
To die with you we will be bound
In hope of salvation
Whatsoever betide.

(The Prophets *cross to* Antichrist)

Enoch: Say, thou very devil's limb
   That sits so grisly and so grim,
   From whom thou came, thou shalt to him,
   For many a soul dost deceive.
   Thou hast deceived men many a day,
   And made the people pay,
   And bewitched them into a wrong way,
   Wickedly with thy wiles.


Antichrist: Ah, false traitors, from me you flee!
   Am not I most in majesty?
   What men dare address them thus to me
   Or keep such distance?


Elias: Fie on thee, traitor, fie on thee!
   Thou art in the devil's fee!
   Through him thou preachest free
   A while, through sufferance.


Antichrist: Oh, you hypocrites that so do cry,
   Lozels! villains! loudly you lie!
   To spill my law you try.
   That speech is good to spare.
   You that my true faith define,
   Mislead these people mine,
   Go out from here and whine.
   To you come sorrow and care!


Enoch: Thy sorrow and care come on thy head!
   For through what thou hast falsely said
   The people is put to pain.
   I would thy body were from thy head
   Twenty miles from it laid
   Till I it brought again.

ANTICHRIST: Out on thee, wizard, with thy wiles!
  For falsely my people thou beguiles:
  I shall see hastily hung.
  And that traitor that stands thee by,
  He puts my folk to great annoy
  With this false flattering tongue.
  But I shall teach you courtesy,
  Your Saviour to know again on high;
  False thieves, with your heresy,
  Now if you dare, abide!

ENOCH: We be no thieves, we thee tell,
  Thou false fiend, coming from hell.
  We have some words thee to tell,
  My fellow and I have no fear.
  We know thy power and thy might
  As we now have told these kings aright.
  We are now ready with thee to fight
  And all men now may hear.

ANTICHRIST: My might is most, I tell to thee;
  I died, I rose as I did foresee.
  This these Kings saw too with their eye
  And every man and wife.
  And miracles and marvels I did also;
  I counsel you therefore, both fall low
  To worship me and not my foe,
  And let us no more strive.

ELIAS: They were no miracles, but marvellous things
  That thou shewedst to these kings;
  Into falsehood thou them brings
  Through the fiend's craft.
  And as the flower now springs,
  Falls, fades and on the ground it clings,
  So thy joy now it reigns
  And soon will you have left.

ANTICHRIST: My curse I give you to amend your ways,
From your head unto your heels!
Out on you, thieves, why fare you thus?
Which would you rather have: pain or bliss?
I may save you from all amiss;
I made the day and also the night,
And all things that are on earth growing,
Flowers fresh that fair can spring;
Also I made every other thing,
And stars that be so bright.


ELIAS: Thou liest! vengeance on thee befall!
Out on thee, wretch! vex thee I shall;
Thou call'st thee king and lord of all—
A fiend is thee within.


ANTICHRIST: Thou liest falsely, I thee tell;
Thou shalt be damned into hell;
I made the man of flesh and fell,
And all that is living.
For other gods have you none,
Therefore worship me alone,
Who hath made the water and stone
And all at my liking.


Wretches, fools, you are blind;
God's son I am, from Him sent;
How dare you maintain your intent
Since He and I are one?
Have I not, since I came him from
Made the dead to speak and go?
And to men I send my ghost also
If they believed me upon.


ENOCH: Now of thy miracles would I see.

ELIAS: Therefore come hither are we:
  Do what we may all see,
  And prove the words we hear.

ANTICHRIST: Soon may you see if you will abide.
  For I will neither fight nor chide.
  Of all the world that is so wide
  There is not my peer.

ENOCH: Bring forth those men here in our sight,
  That thou hast raised against the right,
  If thou art so high in might,
  To make them eat and drink.

ANTICHRIST: You dead men, rise, and list to me.
  Come, eat and drink that men may see,
  And prove me worthy of deity
  And help this strife to sink.

1ST DEAD MAN: Lord, thy bidding I will do aye,
  And for to eat I will assay.

2ND DEAD MAN: And I also, all that I may,
  Will do thy bidding here.

ELIAS: Have there bread, both two,
  But I must bless it ere I go
  That the fiend, mankind's foe,
  On it can have no power.
  This bread I bless with my hand,
  In Jesus' name I understand,
  He who is Lord of sea and land,
  And King in Heaven so high.
  " In nomine patris ", that all hath wrought,
  " Et filii virginis " that dear us bought,

" Et spiritus sancti " is all my thought:
One God and Persons three.

1ST DEAD MAN: Alas, put that bread out of my sight!
To look on it I am not light;
That print thou put'st there aright
Drives me to great fear.

2ND DEAD MAN: To look on it I am not light,
That bread to me it is so bright,
And is my foe, both day and night,
And drives me to great fear.

ENOCH: Now, you men that have done amiss,
You see well what his power is.
Convert to Him at once, I wis,
That you on rood bought.

1ST KING: Ah, now we know, openly,
We have been brought to heresy;
With you our death we soon will see
And never after turn our thought.

2ND KING: Now, Enoch and Eli, it is no nay,
You have tainted thy tyrant this same day.
Blessed be Jesu born of a may
'Tis him I believe upon.
Thou traitor, filled with fantasy,          (*To* ANTICHRIST)
With sorcery, witchcraft and necromancy,
Thou hast led into heresy;
Fie on thy works each one!

1ST KING: Jesu, for thy mighty grace,
Forgive us all our trespass,
And bring us to thy heavenly place,
As thou art God and man.

Now am I wise made through thy might;
Blessed be thou, Jesu, day and night!
The grisly anger girds him to fight
To slay us here anon.

ANTICHRIST: Ah, false traitors, turn ye now?
Ye shall be slain, I make a vow,
And those wizards that turned you,
I shall make them die in pain;
That all others, by this sight,
Shall know that I am most of might;
For with this sword now will I fight,
For all you shall be slain.

(ANTICHRIST *slays all with his sword and returns to his throne:*
    MICHAEL *enters*)

ARCHANGEL MICHAEL: Antichrist, now come is thy last day:
Reign no longer now ye may.
He that hath led thee alway
To him now must thou go.
No more men shall be slain by thee;
My Lord wills that dead thou be.
He that hath given this power so free,
To him thy soul I shall throw.

In sin engendered first thou wast,
In sin led thy life thou hast;
In sin an end to it thou putt'st,
For thou'st marred many a one.
Three year and half one, truthfully,
Thou hast had leave to destroy
God's people wickedly,
With false words said.
Now shalt thou know in high
That more is God's mastery
Than even the Devil's and thine can try,
For now thou shalt be dead.

Thou hast ever served Satanas
And had his power in every place,
Therefore now gett'st thou no grace,
With him thou must be gone.

(MICHAEL *kills* ANTICHRIST *who cries* " Help, Help,
Help ")

ANTICHRIST: Help, Satanas and Lucifer,
Beelzebub, bold bachelor!
Ragnel! Ragnel! thou art my dear!
Now fare I wondrous evil!
Alas, alas, where is my power!
Alas, my wits I cannot steer;
Now body and soul, both together,
And all goeth to the Devil!
(*He dies and* TWO DEVILS *run on to the stage*)

1ST DEVIL: Anon, master, anon!
From hellground I heard thee groan;
I thought not to come myself alone,
For respect of thine estate.
With us to Hell thou shalt be gone;
For this death we make great moan,
To win more souls what shall be done?
Now it is too late.

2ND DEVIL: With me thou shalt; from me thou come;
Of me shall come thy last doom,
For thou hast well deserved.
And through me, powerful and mighty,
Thou hast lived in dignity
And many a soul deceived.

1ST DEVIL: This body was gotten, by mine assent,
In clean whoredom, in true intent,
From mother's womb; ere on earth he went
I was him within;

And taught him aye, with my intent,
The sin in which his life was spent;
Because he did my commandment
Now shall his rejoicing begin.

2ND DEVIL: Now, fellow, in faith, great moan we may make
For this lord of estate that lies dead.
Many a fat morsel we had for his sake
On souls that should be saved by him fed.

1ST DEVIL: His soul with sorrow to Hell is now bent,
Yea, penance and pain soon shall he feel;
To Lucifer, that lord, it shall be present,
To burn as a brand, his sorrow shall not cool.

2ND DEVIL: This proctor of prophecy hath procured many a
one
In his laws to believe and be lost for his sake.
Their souls are in sorrow, and shall be soon,
Such masteries through my might do I make.
(ENOCH *and* ELIAS *begin to recover*)

1ST DEVIL: With Lucifer that lord long shall he linger;
In a seat full of sorrow with him shall he sit.

2ND DEVIL: Yea, by the heels in Hell shall he hang,
In a dungeon deep, right in hell pit.

1ST DEVIL: To hell will I hie, without any fail,
With this present of price thither to bring.

2ND DEVIL: Take thou him by the top and I by the tail;
A sorrowful song, in faith, shall he sing.

1ST DEVIL: Ah, fellow, a doleful look now thou deal
To all this fair company, ere hence thou wend.

2ND DEVIL: Yea, sorrow and care ever shall they feel;
   All sinful shall dwell in hell at their last end.

(Exeunt carrying ANTICHRIST)

ENOCH: Ah, Lord, that all the world shall lead
   And judge the quick and dead,
   That reverence thee to them good read
   And them through right relieve.
   I was dead and right here slain,
   But through thy might, Lord, and thy main,
   Thou hast raised me up again;
   Thee will I love and believe.

ELIAS: Yea, Lord, blessed may thou be!
   My flesh now glorified I see;
   Against thee no treachery
   Conspired may be in any way.
   All that believe in thee steadfastly,
   Thou helpest, Lord, from all annoy,
   For dead I was and now live I;
   Lord, honoured be thou aye!

MICHAEL: Enoch and Elias, come you anon.
   My Lord wills that you with me be gone
   To Heaven's bliss both blood and bone,
   Evermore there to be.
   You have been long—for you be wise—
   Dwelling in earthly paradise;
   But to Heaven, where Himself is,
   Now shall you go with me.

(Leads ENOCH and ELIAS up to Heaven)

END OF SIXTEENTH PLAY

## 17. The Last Judgement

GOD THE FATHER: I God, greatest of degree,
   For whom no beginning could be,
   The Master over land and sea
   As clearly may be proved,
   In my Godhead are persons three
   All of us indivisible be
   And that sovereign right that is in me
   To others may be moved.
   It is an age since I in my might
   Did make a reckoning of the right.
   Now to the doom I set my sight
   That the dead shall truly dread.
   Therefore, my angels, fair and bright
   Look that you wake up each worldly wight
   That they may all come into my light,
   All those for whom I bled.

1ST ANGEL: Lord, that madest through thy might,
   Heaven and earth, day and night,
   Without distance, swift as light
   Your bidding shall be done.
   Straight to awake each worldly wight
   I shall be ready upon this height,
   To show them forth into thy sight
   And them you shall see soon.

           (ANGELS *blow their trumpets*)

1ST POPE: While I lived in flesh and blood,
   Thy great Godhead that is so good
   I never knew although I should,
   Thy worship to begin.
   The wits, Lord, thou sent to me
   I used to come to great degree;

The highest office under thee
On earth thou puttest me in.
When I on earth was at my own will
The world did blind and call me still,
But thy commandments to fulfil
I was full negligent.
But purged it is with pains ill
In Purgatory that sore can grill
Yet with thy grace here on this hill
I stand after great torment.


1ST EMPEROR: Ah, Lord and sovereign saviour
That placed me living in great honour
And made me king and emperor
Highest of kith and kin;
My flesh, lying fallen as the flower
Thou hast restored now by thy power
And with pains and great langour
Cleansed me of my sin.
In Purgatory my soul hath been
A thousand years in pain so keen
Till there is no sin upon me seen:
Purged to be one of thine.
Though I was for riches renowned
And all my days to sin was bound,
Yet at the last contrition me found
And now I stand in thy line.


1ST QUEEN: While I on earth all rich could go
I dressed in satin and silk also
And velvet too that brought me woe
With all such other weeds
That all might excite lechery;
Pearls and other jewellery
Against thy bidding used I,
And other wicked deeds.

Neither prayed I, nor ever fast;
Save alms deeds if any passed;
And great repentance at the last
Which has brought me to thy grace.
Now saved I hope for ever to be
For the cleansed sins that were in me.
Thy last judgement may I not flee
But come now before thy face.                    (*The Damned enter*)


2ND POPE: Alas, O woe is me, alas!
Now am I worse than ever I was;
My body has taken my soul, alas,
That long has been in hell.
Together they stay, I have no grace,
Defiled they look before my face,
And after my death here in this place
In pain for ever to dwell.
Now bootless it is to ask mercy
For, living, highest in earth was I
For my knowledge chosen in papacy
But covetousness did me tear.
Also silver and simony
Made me Pope full unworthy.
They burn me now full bitterly
For of bliss I am quite bare.
Of all souls in Christianity
That were damned while I held the See.
Now to give account behoveth me
Through my lapses forlorn.
Also damned now must I be,
Before I can elsewhere flee:
Make me dead I conjure thee,
As though I had never been born.


2ND EMPEROR: Alas, oh world, why went I there?
Alas, that ever my mother me bare.

Of all this woe I must work my share,
Escape can I not this chance.
Alas, do evil, who is there that dare?
We can protest no more against this care
For to feel pain we ordained are
For ever without deliverance.
Now is manslaughter upon me seen,
Now covetousness makes my pains more keen,
Now wrong-working, secret unseen,
All in the world have I wrought.
Misgotten money I revelled among
And now I am in the hellish throng
Hurt, burnt and whipped by the deadly thong.
In pain I for ever am caught.

2ND QUEEN: Alas, that I was woman wrought!
Alas, that God me out of naught
And with his precious blood me bought
To work against his will!
Lechery I never wrought
But ever to do that sin I sought
And of filth in deed and thought
I had never yet my fill.
Fie on pearls, fie on pride,
Fie on gowns! They may not abide.
Fie on beauty which quickly has died!
These have harrowed me in hell.
Against my lot I may not chide.
This bitter chance I must abide
Of woe and dread suffer the tide
Which no living tongue can tell.
(JESUS *descends*: ANGELS *bring the instruments of the Passion*)

JESUS: You good and evil, that here are sent;
Here you come to your judgement:
Now you will learn what is for you meant
And in what manner.

And all mine, on goodness bent,
Prophets, patriarchs here present
Must know my word with good intent
Therefore I am now here.

But you shall hear and see no less
That I give you all in righteousness;
Charitable deeds, both more and less
I will recall now here.
Of earth through me man made thou was
And put in place of great fineness,
From which straight through wickedness
Away thou hastened there.

After dying on the rood tree
And my blood shedding as thou mayst see
To deprive the devil of all ye
And win ye all away,
That selfsame blood, behold all ye,
Still remembered now it should be
For these good reasons that I offer ye
Of which I will now say.

One cause was this certainly
That to my Father almighty
At my ascension offer might I
This blood craving a boon:
That he of you should have mercy
And more gracious therafter be,
Though you had all sinned horribly
Not taking vengeance too soon.

1ST POPE: Ah, Lord, though I lived in sin
In Purgatory I have long been,
Suffering so long with fire and din
To bring me at last to bliss.

1ST EMPEROR: Yes, Lord, and therein have I be
   More than three hundred years and three;
   Now I am clean, forsake not me,
   Although I did amiss.


1ST QUEEN: And I, Lord, to thee cry and call,
   Thine own Christian now and thrall,
   That of my sins am purged all,
   Of thy joy I thee pray.


JESUS: Come hither to me, my darlings dear,
   That blessed in the world always were;
   Take my realm, all together
   That for you ordained is.
   For while I was on earth here
   You gave Me meat in good manner,
   Therefore in Heaven bliss clear
   You shall forever have, I wis.
   In thirst you gave me to drink,
   When I was naked also clothing
   And when I needed harbouring
   You kept me out of the cold.
   And other deeds to my liking
   You did on earth while living;
   Therefore you shall be quit your sin
   And receive back a hundredfold.


   Therefore, my angels, go you anon
   And take my chosen, everyone
   And show them where they shall be gone
   To live for aye in bliss.
   On my right hand they shall be set
   For that of yore I promised
   When they did as I to them said
   And lived without amiss.

1ST ANGEL: Lord, we shall never cease,
Till we have brought them to their peace,
Those souls who have gained an eternal lease
In this land as they shall see.

2ND ANGEL: And I know them all, so good and fine
The bodies, Lord, that are all thine;
They shall have joy without repine
And that shall ne'er ended be.

(*They lead off the Saved Souls singing* " Salvator mundi Domine ")

1ST DEVIL: Ah, righteous Judge, with most of might
That are now set to doom aright,
Mercy thou hadst to those bright
To save those good men from repine.
Do as thou hast promised
With those sinful as thou hast said
To our kingdom let them be led
And name these men for mine.
Judge this Pope mine in this place
That is worthy for his great trespass;
Not to be thine through grace
But come through sin to be mine.
This Emperor and Queen would never know
Poor men, them alms to show.
Therefore put them in my row
Where fire shall burn them fine.

2ND DEVIL: Nay, I dispute with him in this
Though he sit as High Justice;
And if I see he is righteous
Soon I shall make assay.
These words, God, thou saidst express
As Matthew beareth witness,

That according as man's deed was,
Rewarded he should be.
And lest thou forget, good man,
I shall recall how the text ran
For speak Latin well I can
And that thou soon shalt see.
Therefore righteous if thou be
These men in this row belong to me;
For one good deed here before thee
They have not come to show.
If there be any, speak on, let us see;
If there be none, condemn them to me,
Or else thou art as false as we
And all men shall well know.

1st DEVIL: Yea, this thou saidst in good intent
That when thou came to judgement
Thy angels from thee should be sent
To part the evil from the good,
And put them into great torment
Where moaning and groaning were fervent.
These words to clerks here present
I will repeat, by the rood:

   " Sic erit in consummatione saeculi; exibunt angeli et
      separabunt malos de medio justorum, et mittent eos
      in caminum ignis, ubi erit fletus et stridor dentium."

Therefore deliver these men
And as I once broke my head
I will make them grin
And ruthfully to cry.
And in as hot a chimney
As is ordained for me,
Baked all shall they be
And in bitter moan shall fry.
This proud Pope here present
For covetousness was always bent

This Emperor died without amendment
Therefore I hold them mine.
This Queen used man's heart to stir
She spared no sin in no manner,
Now she has lost all her allure
She too shall peak and pine,


JESUS: Lo, you men that wicked have been
What Satan sayeth you have heard and seen,
Rightful judgement this has been;
For grace is put away.
When time of grace was lasting
To seek it you had no liking;
Therefore must I in everything
Do righteousness today.
And though my sweet mother dear
And all the saints that ever were
Prayed for you right now here
All that were now too late.
No grace may come through their prayer,
Or righteousness has no power
Therefore go to the fire in fear
You gain no other grace.
When I was hungry and thirsty both
And naked was, you would not Me clothe
And sick and in great woe
You would not visit Me.
Nor yet in prison to come
Nor of your meat give Me some,
Nor shelter give me when I was numb.
Never kind to Me were ye.


2ND POPE: When wast thou naked or harbourless
Hungry, thirsty or in sickness?
Or ever in a prison.  Never, I guess.
See this we never could.

2ND EMPEROR: Had we thee hungry or thirsty seen,
    Naked, sick or in prison been,
    Harbourless or cold by any mean,
    Have helped you be sure we would.

JESUS: Nay, when you saw the least of mine
    That on this earth were forced to pine
    With riches ye never helped them to dine
    To fulfil all my desire.
    And since you would nothing incline
    To help the poorest of mine
    For me your love it was not fine,
    Therefore go to the fire.

1ST DEVIL: Ah, Sir Judge, this goeth aright
    By Mahound much of might,
    You be mine, each wight
    Ever to live in woe.
    A doleful death for you, I say,
    For such as you now I have my way.
    Since you served me both night and day
    You shall be rewarded so.
    Go we forth to hell from high
    Without end there shall ye lie
    For you have lost just as did I
    The bliss that lasteth ever.
    Judged you be into Hell's belly
    Where endless sorrow is nigh
    And one thing I tell you truly;
    Delivered will you be never.        (DEVILS *take them away*)

(THE FOUR EVANGELISTS *enter*)

MATTHEW: I, Matthew, of this bear witness,
    For in my gospel I writ express
    This, that my Lord of His goodness
    Has enacted here.
    All by me were warned before,

To save their souls for evermore,
That through their lives are punished sore
And damned to fire in their fear.

MARK: I, Mark, now openly say,
That they were warned by many a way
How their living they should array
Heaven's bliss to recover.
So that excuse themselves they never may
For they are all worthy, in good fay,
To suffer the doom given this day
And damned to be for ever.

LUKE: And I, Luke, on earth living
My Lord's words in every thing
I wrote all, from my knowing,
That all men know might.
And therefore I say forsooth, I wis,
Excuse for this none there is;
Against my talking they did amiss
This doom it goeth aright.

JOHN: And I, John the Evangelist,
Bear witness of things that I wist
In which they might full well have trust
And not have done amiss.
And all that ever my Lord said here,
I wrote it all in my manner;
Therefore excuse you that stand damned here
I may not well, I wis.

> (*If it is desired, the entire company can be introduced for this play and separated at the Judgement. All who remain after the devils have taken their protesting selection should join in singing a final Alleluia.*)

END OF SEVENTEENTH PLAY

# APPENDIX

## HINTS ON PRODUCTION

THE CHESTER PLAYS are suitable for performance either singly or as a cycle today and a few hints may be given upon the conventions and symbolism which may be employed to set out these plays to their best advantage.

In schools they can make a deep impression with nothing more than the furniture of the room to assist the imagination. In this context medieval plays, as many teachers have found, can be especially happy since they are suitable, by reason of their subject matter, for all school ages. The last two in the present volume are unsuitable for juniors but there is throughout the cycle plenty to sustain the attention of all children. The original communal method of presentation applies today nowhere better than to the different forms in a school and from a study or performance of these plays a study of the medieval town can naturally arise and be linked with other knowledge about the period in English civilisation.

There is another reason for the success of medieval plays with children of about twelve years. At this age children pass through a stage of mental development in which they have an instinctive feeling for dramatisation and approach the familiar biblical scenes in much the same way as did medieval people. Whether or not they are re-enacting the history and feelings of the race is for the psychologists to decide but it has been proved in an experiment that boys can create their own versions of well-known scenes with an eye to effect quite like that of the early dramatist's. On one occasion a class was given the outline of the contents of a nativity sequence and without any prompting they felt that Herod was a comically deflated character, full of empty blustering, in the same way as the authors of such plays as the present. Given this natural inclination towards the drama, the success of medieval plays is assured in class.

To present a cycle is an ambitious undertaking and the best approach today is that drawn from the conventions of medieval French performances. A long platform was erected against a wall in a public square and upon it were placed a succession of small stages or *maisons*. At first these were identified solely by chairs placed at intervals along the stage and then by raising several parts of the stage which were individually curtained and variously furnished to represent a palace, a sepulchre or a stable. Acting took place upon these small stages or in front of them where a delocalised zone could be used for journeys or open spaces. Where it was possible a higher level was reserved for heaven, probably festooned with clouds, and a lower one for hell which might have real fire, a large dragon's mouth and possibly trapdoors on to the stage. With three levels to work upon, a French producer (it is curious to note that he himself, with his book in his hand, is seen in the middle of a performance standing in the centre of the stage in a well-known picture of a French show) could, give intense variety and pace to a swiftly-changing performance. In all these particulars I believe that a modern producer should imitate these conventions of symbolic setting which I have detailed more fully to help him.

It would be ideal to have as many as ten acting areas if a large open-air site can be found for the Chester Plays. A heaven and a hell are the first necessities and then different *maisons* which may be represented by furniture or a curtained stage. In the first we should place Mary at the Annunciation and could return to this for the scene in the house of Martha and Mary, which is separated from it in time by thirty years. If another house could be devised, Simon the Leper could live in it, or else all could be habited in one house.

A garden with a tree is the essential playing area for Adam and Eve. Abraham uses the same place for the sacrifice of Isaac because it is to be used for the crucifixion later and a mystical link between these scenes—the two Adams and the two son-sacrifices—must be clearly shown. This form of symbolical staging is similar from other art-forms in which an incident in the Old Testament is shown to predict another in the New. In the windows of King's College Chapel, Cambridge, this analogy is taken to its fullest extent and the artist employed all possible parallels between events. On our stage with its simultaneous staging this didactic plan can be appreciated if the producer gives these suggestions careful thought. With the Chester Plays the element of instruction is in keeping, but the significance is not to be laboured: if the point is not easily realised the response of the audience is not greatly impaired. John Donne wrote: " We say that Paradise and Calvary tree grew in one place." He implies a possible doubt in his " we say ", but we can show this actually happening on the stage.

A small raised platform becomes an Ark by drawing up on four sides a painted hull during the boat-building soliloquy. It might be possible for the platform to have a ground floor beneath: in this case the sepulchre could be located there for Christ. Since we read in medieval legend of the Ark floating high on the water up to the moon until some of its inhabitants escaped to the moon itself, the platform should be as high as possible. This will allow for a gradual building up to heaven to take place. At the same time the producer should consider working the plays towards the prompt side of the set when man's sin is displayed because the left hand of God is the destination of the damned and there is found the hellmouth.

A Temple is necessary and localised by seats and a painted background. Here we find the merchants, Annas and Caiaphas, and Antichrist who uses the whole set with extreme freedom.

The Stable may be an isolated set or located upon Noah's platform or in Mary's house according to the general outline and flow of the production.

Herod and Pilate can easily live in the same building since their appearances are well spaced. A short return by Christ to Herod's palace during the Passion, when another Herod is reigning, has been omitted here to simplify the staging.

The playing-area nearest the audience, possibly an apron-stage, is suitable for all journeys: Joseph to seek midwives and the Apostles travelling to Jerusalem. These scenes lack a marked setting and use the neutral area quite effectively.

The provision of an adequate Heaven raises a difficulty because it must have a stairway for various ascents and descents. Hell must have its large dragon's mouth at least six feet high to allow the devils to collect Herod, Antichrist and the damned souls with ease.

With these areas at a lucky producer's disposal the most important factor to decide is the speed of the cycle and the manner in which this is deployed over the whole set. It should be realised that with the simultaneous staging we can achieve symbolic effects lacking in pageant performance and show a set teeming with people in a way that was naturally denied the original performers.

One problem demands solution: the change from Lucifer to Satan. At first he and Lightborne are in white angelic costume: later they are black. In one medieval French performance Lucifer was flung over the heavenly battlements and landed in a bale of straw hidden from the audience by bushes. At the moment of his landing a second actor dressed in black ran on to the set and continued the rôle. Perhaps four actors in this case can be accommodated to provide similar excitement.

Since animals are required it may be pointed out that all Noah's beasts were depicted upon painted cards singly or in long strips. This is adequate and pleasing today. The moving star was originally piloted by an angel at Chester and this might also bear repetition. A painted background may be used upon other occasions to denote any place which has not been provided in the lay-out of the stage.

## Acting

An Elizabethan acting convention is suitable for medieval plays since we have no information about the standards of acting in the middle ages. Immense tact and discretion are necessary in handling the more saintly members of the cast: a species of bland unction cannot be tolerated as a simulation of holiness. A warning to this effect should be given more especially to older actresses who can at once ruin the unity of tone by any such falsity. A sincerity without coyness must be insisted upon: religious drama is like the microphone and the camera in detecting the poseur.

## COSTUME

To dress a large cast is an exacting task: the designer must be able to make artistic use of simple materials and also organise a large body of helpers in the same way as the producer himself. If possible the set should be dressed for each play with an eye to its own colour-scheme. Not only the bright, but also the dull colours must be regarded by the designer. Medieval costume is advisable throughout with a number of significant departures from it for special effect. Thus, Adam and Eve require white suits, as does Christ, during the crucifixion. Originally these were made of leather but this is hardly possible in this country because of its prohibitive cost. Annas and Caiaphas may be dressed in modern episcopal clothes and an element of local anti-clericalism is not out of order at all. According to tradition Ham and one of the Magi are both black and this should be observed. For the paradise scene Satan should assume a green cloak and adopt a form of rhythmical movement to go with it and to display any ingenuity devised in the design. God the Father should be the traditional figure in white robes and white beard, especially as in the first play he is the *paterfamilias* in his heavenly home. How long he is to remain on duty in full view of the audience is for the producer to decide. I feel that he should in fact be seen the entire time probably gazing downwards at human follies.

A knowledge of medieval paintings will enable the designer to maintain connection with medieval schemes of colour and will assist him in the robing of the crowd scenes. Angels and apostles have their symbols and should not be forgotten. The angels must be white and winged, though the wings may be restricted to a wire outline pinned to the shoulders. Gabriel carries a lily or a palm for the Annunciation and Michael a suit of armour for the onslaught upon Antichrist and with these emblems they are identified. The Evangelists' symbols are well-known and should not be neglected for their epilogue Matthew (Angel), Mark (Lion), Luke (winged calf), John (Eagle). Peter has his papal keys, Matthew (as an apostle) his purse, Thomas and Philip, builders' squares and James the Great his pilgrim's hat, shell and staff. Judas is always shown with red hair and beard, carrying the purse with the thirty pieces of silver; his costume is always yellow. Medieval audiences would have spotted these symbols and emblems and it is surely necessary to adhere to these traditions.

One detail concerning Antichrist may be mentioned. For some years the present writer has been puzzled by a line in Ben Jonson's *Alchemist* where the Puritan Ananias remarks to a character in Spanish disguise: " Thou lookest like Antichrist in that lewd hat! " Finding at last two medieval pictures of Antichrist I believe that this enigmatic man was presented always in a hat, where Christ had none, and that it was a bishop's skull-cap with a central stalk and a band round the forehead that was chosen. Thus Antichrist reminded Ananias of a Catholic bishop (it cannot be said that the upper hierarchy comes well out of this cycle) and he should retain this distinction in costuming today.

An outdoor performance with a large cast raises certain problems for the designer that are absent in the theatre. A basic medieval dress should be drawn up from a pattern and a prototype made. Copies of this can then be taken without difficulty and only in colour need any difference be made. The materials employed are of some importance since textures themselves become a kind of social distinction: the crowd should wear cloth which may retain rough edges and have a matt surface, the gentry should have a finer texture. In order to dress a large crowd economically it is advisable to buy a long roll of white material wholesale and cut it into lengths for dyeing and working. In this way simple dresses can be put together for about ten shillings and more complicated ones from about fifteen shillings, though these prices are approximations. Advice upon the basic patterns and many aspects of costuming a medieval play will be found in:

IRIS BROOKE, *Medieval Theatre Costume* (A. & C. Black)

## MUSIC

The arrangement of the music for a mystery cycle is also a highly specialised undertaking because medieval music itself is known only to scholars. Music should be employed throughout the cycle and the angelic chorus should be the main source, for they are called upon to sing frequently. I have not always specified in the text the portions that can be set to music because the decision lies with the musical director and the amount of suitable vocal and instrumental work he can provide. Noah and Christ sing at different stages and the important acting trios can also sing if desirable. Plain chant will provide settings for Latin songs mentioned in stage-directions though English words should be used as often as possible. The best source of all such vocal music is now the volume of medieval Carols edited by John Stevens and published by the Royal Musical Association in its series *Musica Britannica*[1]. The selection will be difficult as so many of the carols deserve to be heard by a choir and the musical director will be loath to part with many of these strong settings of appropriate words. The Oxford Book of Carols is not so authentic as Dr. Stevens's edition and should be used with care. The work of David Munrow and his Early Music Consort must also be mentioned as modern realisations of old music that have immense vitality and will be of value to the producer.

At certain points in the cycle passages of instrumental music might be used; this need be not medieval provided that

---

[1] Obtainable from Messrs Stainer and Bell Ltd., 29 Newman Street, London, W.1.

there is power and brilliance in it. Original music, if it can be composed, will be an excellent prologue before the first speech and to special music we should return at the Nativity, at the Crucifixion and at the Judgement. Here some strident music is necessary to suggest the terrors of Hell which cannot be shown in any way upon the stage and to account for the reluctance of the victims. A final alleluia from all survivors is an essential in closing the whole cycle; this too may be an original composition. To demand a great quantity of music is impossible and the choice and provision of it will rest with the musical director and producer. It is hoped, however, that no familiar music will be heard during the performance of the cycle since that will help to render the undertaking familiar and remove the experience of wonder and mystery that a medieval cycle should have for us today. A cycle is an artistic experience fashioned out of a past world and this should never be out of the minds of organisers or performers.

Whether these plays are given in a classroom, a small or large theatre, a garden, a church or in any outdoor place in which different levels can be marked with walls, bushes, trees or platforms they should be deeply moving if the producer is assured of the artistic integrity of the cycle he is mounting and the traditional value of what he is repeating. It is hoped that the above notes may be of some use to those who are not already accustomed to the symbolic staging of medieval drama, and that they may lead them to a slightly closer approximation to the original form of these entertainments, which, as Professor Salter has remarked: " come to us encrusted with the living and thinking of real people, dwelling in real towns, experiencing plague and pestilence, rain and sunshine, revelry and tragedy, life, birth, marriage, child-bearing and decrepitude through generation after generation of brief lives ".